"Although the editors refer to this volume as a 'Little Book' (because of its length), there is nothing 'little' about the ideas it espouses. Reading the backgrounds of the authors of the letters and then the elements they focused on in their visit to Singapore is an engaging experience. Our Massachusetts educators, scholars, and practitioners that traveled to Singapore have provided unique insight into the tremendous educational progress that has occurred in Singapore and the lessons that will serve us well as we attempt to fully align all segments of education in the Commonwealth for the benefit of our citizens."

Carlos E. Santiago, Massachusetts Commissioner of Higher Education

"This book represents well both the advantages and disadvantages of the Singapore education system and its plan for developing excellent educators and education leaders. It is a very helpful document for higher education and policy leaders."

Marty Meehan, President, University of Massachusetts

This book is a valuable and compelling account of what Singapore has done to build teaching into a robust profession in the 21st century. Developing solid foundations and systems to increase teaching professionalism is an imperative of our time, critical to offering all children a relevant education of high quality. Those interested in strengthening the teaching profession would benefit from reading this engaging book.

James E. Ryan, Dean of the Faculty and Charles William Eliot Professor, Harvard Graduate School of Educat

"Cheers to Reimers and his team for an insightful ' Singapore and how that small country can be educators and policymakers. Fifteen Letters is in improving American education for the 21st C

Anthony J. Bent, Chair, Global Stu   Century Skills Committee and past President, Massa usetts Association of Schools Superintendents and former Superintendent of Shrewsbury Public Schools, Massachusetts

Fifteen Letters on Education in Singapore is an outstanding contribution to the literature on school improvement. The writing is brisk and the policy recommendations for US schools are practical. This is indispensable reading for everyone who cares about transforming and uplifting education for all students."

Dennis Shirley, Professor, Lynch School of Education, Boston College

"Fernando Reimers' beautifully written Introduction describes how *Fifteen Letters* evokes the manner in which John Quincy Adams' observations on Prussian education were captured and shared through his Letters on Silesia, which subsequently influenced the origins of public education in America. Drawing on this reference, *Fifteen Letters* is a masterful orchestration that provides us with one of the most authentic renderings of contemporary experiential learning in this context. Learning through the eyes of others in this way made for a fascinating read especially on such a riveting topic as education in Singapore."

Bella Wong, Superintendent, Lincoln-Sudbury Regional School System, Massachusetts

"For educators, policy makers, and other stakeholders seeking answers to essential educational questions, these letters are a must read. While learning about the strengths of Singapore's system, whether it is the collaborative spirit and reflective nature of its educators or the value the nation places on the teaching profession, the reader is left with a sense of hopefulness. This book shows that we have much to learn from others."

Jeff Shea, Social Studies Teacher Belmont High School and Massachusetts Teacher of the Year 2015

"This economical, refreshing book on Singapore's world-beating education system incorporates multiple perspectives from various educators who examine Singapore's success, distill its key features and speculate on the application of these elements to the US system. It's a quick, informative and stimulating read for anyone interested in the potential application of international lessons for US schools."

Paul Reville, Francis Keppel Professor of Practice of Educational Policy and Administration and Director, Education Redesign Lab, Harvard University Graduate School of Education

"For those of us who have not had the opportunity to see first-hand the acclaimed Singapore school system, this book is a perfect choice. It offers a variety of intriguing perspectives from insightful educators—complimentary and critical—determined to mine what we can learn from Singapore to improve America's schools."

Ron Berger, Chief Academic Officer, EL Education

"Just as our first graders move in the student-centered classroom from one learning station to the next, and as our teachers investigate and collaborate across classrooms and districts, so do the authors of *Fifteen Letters* explore schools throughout Singapore to learn and to understand other viewpoints and methods that hold the potential to reshape education policy at the highest levels in American education. Learn with them as you move form perspective to perspective hearing their thoughts."

Paul Dakin, Superintendent of Schools, Revere, Massachusetts

"As a teacher whose learning and advocacy experiences span from the classroom all the way to the U.S. Department of Education, I can attest to the value of diverse perspectives and purposeful reflection. And yet, as any educator knows, action must follow reflection in order to create change. This book not only offers diverse perspectives about Singapore's education system, or reflective discussion of implications; it provides direct recommendations for action at all levels of the education system (from the classroom all the way to the DE)."

Audrey Jackson, 5th Grade Inclusion Teacher, Joseph P. Manning Elementary School, Jamaica Plain, Massachusetts and Massachusetts Teacher of the Year 2016

FIFTEEN LETTERS on EDUCATION in SINGAPORE

Reflections from a Visit to Singapore in 2015 by a Delegation of Educators from Massachusetts

Edited by Fernando M. Reimers and E. B. O'Donnell
with contributions from
Lisa Battaglino, Connie K. Chung, Mitalene Fletcher,
David Harris, Joey Lee, Vanessa Lipschitz, Ee-Ling Low,
David Lussier, Christine McCormick, Meghan O'Keefe,
Oon-Seng Tan, Paul F. Toner, and Eleonora Villegas-Reimers

ISBN: 978-1-4834-5062-9 (sc)
ISBN: 978-1-4834-5063-6 (e)

Library of Congress Control Number: 2016906430

Lulu Publishing Services rev. date: 04/25/2016

CONTENTS

Introduction. How learning from Singapore can support improvement at home

by Fernando M. Reimers

The Origins of this Little Book

This publication is the compilation of a series of short reflections from a small group of educators from Massachusetts who travelled together to Singapore to learn about that country's remarkable education journey. Our simple goal in publishing this document is to have a tangible and practical resource we can use to share with colleagues our reflections about lessons learned on that visit, as well as our thoughts about possible implications of Singapore's practice for educators in Massachusetts.

The background of this project is simple. As part of a research project on 21st century education[1] I lead at Harvard University, the Global Education Innovation Initiative[2], I had been studying the strategic, pragmatic, and successful approach Singapore's education leaders followed to build a high quality education system over the course of the country's short history. In the context of our research collaboration, I invited some of my colleagues at Singapore's National Institute of Education (NIE) to participate in a policy roundtable at Harvard. I also invited to this event a number of education leaders from Massachusetts, including the Commissioner of Elementary and Secondary Education and some of his senior staff, members of the state board of higher education, leaders of several teacher education institutions, among others. There was real interest at that meeting in the way in which Singapore had professionalized the teaching force and in how they prepared school leaders, two strategies that made up their basic approach to improving education quality.

---

[1] Reimers, F. and Chung, C. (Editors) (2016). *Teaching and Learning in the Twenty First Century*. Cambridge, MA: Harvard Education Press.

[2] To learn more, about this initiative, please visit: http://globaled.gse.harvard.edu/.

Paul Toner, a fellow member of the State Board of Higher Education and former President of the Massachusetts Teacher Association, suggested that we should find a way to follow this meeting up with a visit to Singapore so that we could examine "up close" some of the educational programs and practices our colleagues had described. I reached out to Professor Oon-Seng Tan, Director of Singapore's National Institute of Education, who enthusiastically responded to our request, and agreed to host us for a visit that would help us meet with colleagues directly involved in programs of teacher and principal preparation, visit the NIE, visit schools and other education institutions, and talk to school principals and teachers. We then approached Kate Berseth, Vice President of Education First, an education company that specializes in student and educator international travel, and she and her colleagues agreed to work with us to organize this visit. Finally, we approached Nick Donohue, President of the Nellie Mae Education Foundation, who provided financial support for the visit. We then worked with the Massachusetts Department of Elementary and Secondary Education to invite deans of large teacher preparation programs in the state, district leaders, and other individuals working in teacher education to participate in the trip. Finally, in October of 2015 we went to Singapore where we spent a week talking with colleagues at the National Institute of Education, at the Singapore's Teachers Union, and at various schools.

Throughout the trip, I kept thinking about how valuable international travel was to broaden one's understanding of the educational enterprise and how to improve it. In our last day in Singapore, I reminded the members of our group that such international exchange of ideas had been critical to the establishment of the American education system. John Quincy Adams, the sixth president of the United States, wrote admiringly about the education system of Prussia while he served as ambassador there in his *Letters on Silesia,* a book that helped many of his contemporaries in the United States learn about Prussia's early system of public education. Similarly, Horace Mann, the first Secretary of Education of Massachusetts, wrote a book analyzing the education systems of Germany and France, which helped advance his campaign for public education in the United States[3]. Inspired by *Letters on Silesia*, I asked my fellow travelers whether they would be open to writing "Letters on Singapore." All agreed—I suspect it was as much because they saw potential value in the idea as because it gave us an opportunity to continue our collaboration upon return from this trip. We had greatly enjoyed learning together and from one another in Singapore.

The Role of Comparison and Exchange of Ideas in the Advancement of Public Education

The process of comparison is central to how we make sense of the world. Comparisons, of events that precede and follow other events, of outcomes associated with other events and various conditions, are central to helping us interpret the world, to identify regularities, to generate hypotheses, and to test ideas about causes and effects, in short to describe and to understand the world. The scientific method, a powerful approach that disciplines the human mind in interpreting the world, is essentially a system of rules so that these comparisons are carried away in a manner that can yield intersubjective agreement about the interpretations of the phenomena under study. Comparisons are done in the physical sciences, as well as in the social sciences. Many social sciences—including psychology, anthropology, sociology, and political science—have a comparative subfield that is concerned with the systematic study of similarities and differences across cultures of the particular objects of study of the discipline. This is the case with comparative psychology, sociology, political science, or anthropology.

While education is a profession as well as a science, efforts to build the knowledge base that informs the practice of education have also included the systematic study of comparisons. One of the early

---

[3] Adams, John Quincy. (1804). *Letters on Silesia, written during a tour through that country in the years 1800, 1801*. London, Printed for J. Budd.

proponents of the scientific study of education, Marc Antoine Jullien, proposed two forms of comparative study to inform the enterprise. The first is the study of various pedagogical approaches which existed in his time as well as the systematic exchange of the ideas emerging from those studies among researchers, practitioners and decision makers. The second form is a systematic survey of the organization of schools in different jurisdictions[4]. What is most remarkable about Jullien's ideas, is that he proposed them in the late 18th century—precisely at the time that many nations in Europe engaged in the creation of their public education systems. Jullien might have had in mind that the ambitious undertaking of building such public systems might benefit from a scientific foundation, and that comparisons would have only made the science better.

Much of the comparative knowledge which informed the early creation of public education systems travelled not only in the form of books or letters, but in the stories of travelers who individually and in groups took observations about educational practice from one place to another or travelled to disseminate their methods. Jullien himself, an admirer of the educational method developed by Johann Heinrich Pestalozzi, travelled to study the various institutes that had been established by Pestalozzi and his followers. Pestalozzi himself—who had developed an approach to education based on the revolutionary idea that children are not little adults, that development takes place in stages, and that education should be tailored to the particular stage of the learner—travelled to advocate for his ideas[5]. In 1804 he travelled to Paris to visit Napoleon in hopes of persuading the general of the merits of his approach, as the institute Pestalozzi had established in Burgdorf was in jeopardy as a result of reforms adopted by the Swiss government under Napoleon's influence. Given that one of Pestalozzi's insights was that

---

[4] Delieuvin, Marie-Claude. (2003). *Marc-Antoine Jullien, de Paris, 1775-1848: théoriser et organiser l'éducation*. Paris: Harmattan.
[5] Pestalozzi, J. H. (1827). *Letters on early education: addressed to J.P. Greaves, Esq.* London: Sherwood, Gilbert and Piper.

the goal of education should be to foster the development of the full range of dimensions of the human personality, it is unfortunate that he was unsuccessful in persuading Napoleon of the merit of his approach. Public education around the world might be more comprehensive today than it is had Pestalozzi succeeded.

In contrast, the educational ideas of a contemporary of Pestalozzi, another global traveler, Joseph Lancaster, achieved more global influence—arguably because in 1808 Lancaster and his associates created an organization, the "Society for Promoting the Lancasterian System for the Education of the Children of the Poor," to disseminate his method. Lancaster established a free elementary school in Southwark, England, in 1798, and in 1803 published a book describing the method *Improvements in Education*. He traveled widely to lecture on his ideas and to assist in the establishment of schools adopting the monitorial method which would serve as teacher training centers. In 1818 he helped to establish a school in Philadelphia. He also helped establish schools in Baltimore (United States), Montreal (Canada), Nyon (Switzerland), and Caracas (Venezuela). His followers established schools in Bogota (Colombia), Quito (Ecuador), Lima (Peru) and in numerous cities in Mexico. At the time of Lancaster's death about 1300 schools used his method.

Lancaster's method was simple: as a way to extend the reach of education to a larger number of children, which in his time largely depended on instruction provided by highly qualified tutors, Lancaster proposed developing clarity on the educational goals of a course of study and structuring such course in a modular sequence so that different modules could be taught by more advanced students—referred to as monitors—under the supervision of a single tutor who could in this way oversee an entire school[6]. This method, which was really aimed at teaching a limited

---

[6] Lancaster, J. (1833). *Epitome of some of the chief events and transactions in the life of Joseph Lancaster, containing an account of the rise and progress of the Lancasterian system of Education.* New Haven: Printed for the author by Baldwin & Peck; New York, Carvill & Co.

range of competencies to large groups of children at low cost, was especially appealing to reformers, particularly given the low cost per student. The method also proved very congruent with the "one room school," the emerging form of organization in several parts of the world in his time. The monitorial system was developed concurrently and independently by Lancaster and by Dr. Andrew Bell in Madras, India, who based the 'Madras System of Education' on his observations of traditional games in India which enabled children to learn from their peers[7].

The educational travels and comparative observations of Horace Mann and, before him, John Quincy Adams have been mentioned above. It was likely the cumulative impact of educational ideas and comparisons of these sorts that shaped much of the discourse that supported the development of public education in the United States in the first century of the republic.

Similar educational comparisons and exchanges of educational practices happened elsewhere. Francisco de Miranda, one of the leaders of the independence movement of South America and another global traveler, visited the United States to learn about a series of educational institutions and their role in the creation of the new republic. Thanks to letters of introduction from Benjamin Franklin, Miranda visited the Presidents of Yale and Harvard Colleges, and wrote admiringly of the libraries of both institutions in his diary. Miranda lived for years in London, where he had met Joseph Lancaster, and promptly introduced Lancaster to a delegation of fellow Venezuelans who visited soon after that nation had achieved independence: Simón Bolívar, Andrés Bello and Luis López Méndez. Bolivar brought Lancaster to Venezuela a few years later to begin the first teacher education institution in that country[8].

---

[7] Hollingsworth, N. J. (1812). *An address to the public, in recommendation of the Madras system of education : as invented and practised by the Rev. Dr. Bell ... with a comparison between his schools and those of Mr. Joseph Lancaster.* London : Printed by Law and Gilbert.

[8] Fernández Heres, R. (1984). *Sumario sobre la escuela caraqueña de Joseph Lancaster (1824-1827).* San Cristóbal [Venezuela]: Universidad Católica del Tachira (Colección Sumario ; 9).

Travel and exchanges of that sort have been common since the creation of public education—and even before. Domingo Faustino Sarmiento, an Argentinean educator, was travelling in Europe to study the education system of those nations, when he happened upon a just published copy of *The Common School*. He immediately travelled to Boston, curious to meet the author, Horace Mann. Sarmiento first met Harvard professor Henry Longfellow, in his house on Brattle Street in Cambridge. Longfellow referred Mann to Sarmiento, and Sarmiento went to Concord where he would meet Mann and his wife, Mary Tyler Peabody Mann. Upon his return to South America, Sarmiento wrote a book, *Popular Education*, which was undoubtedly influenced by the conversations he had with the Manns and his reflections on the American early experience with public education. Sarmiento would, in time, become Secretary of Education and President of Argentina, and his ideas would provide the foundation for the establishment of public education in South America. The correspondence which Sarmiento and Mary Peabody Mann sustained over more than twelve years is testimony to the power of such exchanges in shaping the educational and cultural institutions of the new republics in the Americas. The letters of Mary Peabody Mann contain explicit suggestions and assistance for developing public schools (as well as an astronomical observatory) in Argentina, and she played a key role in shipping a contingent of teachers from Massachusetts to teach in Argentina, as well as sending the founder of the first astronomical observatory to that country[9]. As testimony of the fruitful friendship that Sarmiento enjoyed with many important leaders in the Commonwealth, his statue sits on Commonwealth Avenue, between Hereford Street and Gloucester Street in Boston.

At the time of the establishment of Teachers College in the early 1900s, the president of Columbia University recognized the importance of comparative study in supporting a more effective practice of education.

---

[9] Velleman, B. (2001). My dear sir : Mary Mann's letters to Sarmiento, 1865-1881. Argentina: Instituto Cultural Argentino Norteamericano.

Of particular interest at the time was how to support teachers who would have to educate students whose parents had not themselves received much schooling. The leaders at Teachers College thought that the comparative study of other education systems would expand the range of ideas and practices used to educate such diverse group of students, many of them immigrants or the children of immigrants. It was for this reason that the International Institute was established at Teachers College. One of the better known faculty associated with the institute was John Dewey, a global traveler and comparative educator who drew many insights from his travels and the study of education systems in societies as different as China, Mexico, Russia, and Turkey. Another faculty associated with the International Institute was Professor Isaac Kandel, a comparative educator who wrote books on the education systems of several European nations and who was an early proponent of the systematic study of global affairs in high school. In a speech to the association of secondary school principals in 1928, Kandel made a lucid case for the integration of global studies to the curriculum of high schools.

It was in the 1960s that a group of comparative educators, led by Torsten Husén, argued for the launching of a systematic comparative study of education systems—in this way creating the International Association for the Evaluation of Educational Achievement (IEA). Husén's idea was that the world is a much larger laboratory in which to examine variation in educational practices and outcomes than any educational system in a local or national jurisdiction. Over the last five decades, the IEA has broadened the scientific foundation of education through comparative research on the teaching of reading, mathematics, science, and civic education. More recently, in the year 2000, the Organization of Economic Cooperation and Development (OECD), began to conduct similar periodic assessments of student knowledge and skills (the PISA studies) which have further advanced our understanding of global variation in educational outcomes and practices, and has generated many insights from the study of such variation.

This history of educational comparisons and exchange of ideas suggests that education is a global undertaking, and is becoming increasingly so. Not only in that there is much to be gained from learning from the rest of the world, but also in knowing that there is a fraternity of educators that is united by common educational aspirations, even across national boundaries. I have elsewhere argued that a Global Education Movement emerged at the end of World War II, and this movement has produced one of the most remarkable transformations in history, providing most children in the world the opportunity to go to school[10].

Envoy

This is the simple story of how we came to write this little book, and some of the ideas that inspired the undertaking. Upon our return from Singapore, we met again, as we had done before and during our trip, to discuss what we were learning and what we thought might be done differently in our state to improve the quality and relevance of our schools. We agreed that there would be value in publishing these letters as they have been authored by each traveler; we thought the collection of impressions and reflections of the diverse individuals in our group expressed a richness of views that would be lost if we tried to consolidate our observations into a consensus document, written in a single voice. This is the reason we provide a biography for each author of each letter—so that readers can understand what perspective informs each set of observations. We also agreed that we should distill a few takeaways from our reflections and would present those in a single document, the reflection of our collective thinking and work. In this document we present first the collective takeaways, and then the individual letters, although in writing them we each first wrote the letter. I also invited two of our colleagues at the National Institute of Education, Director Professor Oon-Seng Tan, and Director of Strategic Initiatives, Professor Ee-Ling Low, to add their reflections

---

[10] Reimers, F. (2015). Educating the children of the poor: A paradoxical global movement. In Tierney, W. (Ed). *Rethinking Education and Poverty*. Baltimore: Johns Hopkins University Press.

to our document, as we thought the voices of two of the key actors in that system with their extensive knowledge about Singapore's education, would enhance the collection. They did not participate in drafting the take away lessons for Massachusetts.

We hope those of you reading this publication will find value both in the consolidated synthesis of takeaways, as well as in the collection of individual observations which ground the takeaways. We are publishing this book under the least restrictive Creative Commons license to facilitate wide dissemination and utilization of the ideas contained here. To make access to this book possible at low cost, we are publishing it at no profit to the authors in paper copy and electronically. We hope some of our readers will use this book to co-construct with us ways forward for education in Massachusetts. For example, those working in teacher preparation institutions might discuss the ideas contained in this book with colleagues, address the implication of these ideas for their practice and develop action steps specifically for their institution. They could then publish their own version of a book, starting with their own analysis and action steps, incorporating as much of the content of this book into their own as desirable, which the Creative Commons license would allow. The www.glasstree.com platform will facilitate publishing of these derivative works. In this way, we hope to stimulate wide dialogue and collective action leading to co-construction of institution-specific action steps that help us achieve common purpose in professionalizing teaching and in improving the opportunities for students to develop the competencies that matter in the 21st century.[11]

---

[11] The following works explain how broad social dialogue, collective intelligence and improvement networks support adaptive educational change: Reimers, F. and Villegas-Reimers, E. 2014. Getting to the Core and Evolving the Education Movement to a System of Continuous Improvement. *New England Journal of Public Policy*. Fall/Winter 2014. Vol26. Issue 1. Pp. 186-205; Reimers, F. 2014. How ideas matter for Education. Unicef. The State of the World's Children. http://sowc2015.unicef.org/stories/how-ideas-matter-to-advance-equity-in-education/; Reimers, F. and N. McGinn *Informed Dialogue. Changing Education Policies Around the World*. Praeguer Publishers. 1997.

In our various roles as educators, and as a group, we will participate in some of those conversations. We hope the ideas in this book will take a life of their own and inspire debate, creation and action by others that result in improvement in public education. If these reflections have this effect, as the reflections of previous fellow travelers did for public education around the world, we would have achieved our purpose in writing them.

IMPLICATIONS FOR EDUCATOR PREPARATION AND SUPPORT IN MASSACHUSETTS

Fernando M. Reimers, Lisa Battaglino, Connie K. Chung, Mitalene Fletcher, David Harris, Joey Lee, Vanessa Lipschitz, David Lussier, Christine McCormick, E. B. O'Donnell, Meghan O'Keefe, Paul F. Toner, and Eleonora Villegas-Reimers

Upon returning from the visit to Singapore, the participants in the delegation identified a number of possible implications of what we learned for policy and practice in Massachusetts. The central lessons we drew from our visit center around the power of a clear, bold and concise vision; commitment to implementation; the importance of coherence and alignment to implement that vision; and the crucial role of ubiquitous opportunities to build capacity of teachers and other educators. Massachusetts could deepen the effectiveness of its education reform efforts as a result of being more intentional with regards to these four Cs:

> Clear and Bold Vision
> Commitment to Implementation
> Coherence
> Capacity

All of which would help us act more systemically, guided by long-term goals.

In this section we explain each of these four themes, and then develop specific implications of each theme for six stakeholder groups which are central in the design and implementation of education transformation: policy makers, state and district leaders, teacher education institutions, school principals, teachers, and the public.

Clear and bold vision

Real clarity about the intended goals of compulsory education from pre-school to high school[12] is critical for success. This is because goals provide direction to the many individuals who participate in sustaining effective instruction. Clear goals are, in effect, the glue that holds the system together while providing direction that results in powerful, sustained learning for students. Education goals are structured in hierarchies that go from the most specific learning goals for a lesson, to the broader goals of what social good should result from having school graduates master particular competencies. There should be clarity and shared vision about those goals and purposes among teachers, school principals, parents, and others who support their work, such as district and state leaders and the general public.

Effective goals should inspire coordinated hard work that results in powerful instruction and deep learning, in the same manner in which a music sheet enables an orchestra to produce beautiful music rather than an incoherent collection of sounds. To be inspiring, those goals should be bold, and they should withstand the "why" test—that is, they should provide clear answers as people ask more than one time "why" about each proposed goal.

We were impressed by the boldness with which Singapore has framed 21ˢᵗ century K-12 curriculum standards as aligned to their aspiration to be an integrated knowledge economy that is positioned for global leadership. We were equally impressed by how a clear set of ambitious goals, reframed and refined at four distinct periods in Singapore's education's history, has enabled their education system to transition from giving few children the opportunity to access school just five decades ago, to an exemplar of comprehensive education for all students today. Singapore's vision is especially compelling because of how concise

---

[12] Such clarity is also essential at the collegiate level, but since our visit focused on the compulsory levels of education, we focus our learnings there.

the vision was for each major stage of education reform, thus providing a level of focus around a specific direction that framed the vision and a clear logic to why this direction/need was most important at the specific time in the country's development.

Commitment to implementation

If there is one feature that distinguishes Singapore's efforts, it is the clear commitment to implementation, to execution. Planning for implementation means more than articulating clear policy goals and strategies, it means developing a roadmap of who is to do what, with what resources, and in what timeframe; translating goals into a real strategy that can guide actions that result in more effective instruction. In Singapore, education policy is not meant to just inspire in the hope that some actions by some people will follow, but instead is meant to guide and support execution by all teachers, in all schools, and in ways that ensure coherence between policy intent and practice.

Such commitment to implementation is essential; without it, policy goals are just unfunded mandates. Commitment to implementation involves not only clear roadmaps and execution strategies, but also adequate budgets and resources in all forms to carry out the actions necessary to produce the results intended by policy. Commitment to implementation also requires attention to strategic communication so that the many stakeholders in the education system can be on the same page. Most importantly, commitment to implementation requires sufficient continuity of efforts and time to allow goals to translate into effective practice.

Coherence

Since goals are only as effective as are the specific actions that they inspire, and since these actions involve multiple interlocutors in the system, it is essential that these different players act in synergistic ways and not at cross-purposes from each other. The alignment of the actions undertaken by different agencies and units in the education system, and by the different teachers that students will come into contact with during their schooling, is what enables students to experience coherent, effective, sustained, and deep opportunities to learn core values and essential skills.

Singapore illustrates how such articulation of the various components of the education system produces results that are greater than the sum of the parts. This coherence is supported by strategic use of communication, as well as deep relationships between schools, the ministry of education, and the National Institute of Education, which are reinforced by frequent rotation of staff among these institutions.

Capacity

Clear goals, especially if they are ambitious, call for levels of effectiveness in practice that are likely to exceed the current capacities of teachers or others who support their work. This is the reason that opportunities for teacher preparation and development are crucial. Effective teaching can only come from sustained commitment to perfecting one's practice, and robust systems of professional development make such opportunities ubiquitous.

Singapore's commitment to ongoing professional development, to purposeful talent management of all human resources in the education system, is at the core of its success. It is the foundation of coherence and the most concrete expression of its commitment to executing education policy goals.

Given these lessons, what specific actions should key stakeholders involved in education reform in Massachusetts advance or sustain that would increase the potential for achieving our education goals? We propose some actions in the following section, grouping them into the four themes just described, for policy makers, state and district leaders, teacher education institutions, school principals, teachers, and the public.

IMPLICATIONS FOR STATE EDUCATION POLICYMAKERS, INCLUDING
LEADERS FROM THE STATE HOUSE, EXECUTIVE OFFICE OF
EDUCATION, THE COMMISSIONERS OF ELEMENTARY AND
SECONDARY EDUCATION AND HIGHER EDUCATION

Clear and bold vision

- Make explicit and communicate broadly the expected goals of K-12 education and explain how they align with a vision for the future of Massachusetts. Articulate ambitious and rigorous goals that describe how education will prepare students for careers, civic engagement, and life, and goals that aim to increase the number of students prepared for college while providing alternative pathways to career success. For example, provide funding and visibility for career and technical education aligned to the needs of employers, including expansion of alternative high school pathways for students who struggle in traditional academic environments.

- The desired learning outcomes should include the multiple competencies—cognitive, intrapersonal, and interpersonal—that are essential for economic and civic participation in the 21st century, as well as the content knowledge to sustain a knowledge economy in Massachusetts. These goals need to be developed at various levels of specificity: (1) at a broad enough level to be communicated widely and understood by all relevant stakeholders, and (2) as curriculum frameworks that can guide the work of districts, teacher education programs, and service providers.

- Implement a communications strategy designed to effectively reach all relevant stakeholders and align their understanding of the expected goals. Help all relevant constituencies understand the difference between goals and curriculum frameworks and assessment instruments, and articulate how the assessment instruments reflect the intended goals. The result of this strategy should be that every constituency understands how they can support teachers and schools in their efforts to help students gain the essential competencies articulated in the goals from their respective sphere of influence.

Commitment to implementation

- Policy shifts should be accompanied by: (1) explicit implementation strategies and plans; (2) budgets which are adequate to translate those plans into activities and produce results; (3) expected implementation timelines that allow enough time for practice to change; (4) clear integration with teacher education programs; and (5) an infrastructure sufficient to sustain focus and adequate follow up.

Coherence

- Incentivize the revision of the existing common frameworks for teacher education institutions so they are aligned with the expected goals of K-12 education. Given the large number of institutions involved in pre-service teacher education in the state, support the articulation of teacher preparation programs, perhaps drawing on the work of the Department of Higher Education in creating transfer pathways across higher education institutions, for example.

Capacity

- Support the development of a robust infrastructure of teacher professional development for practicing teachers aligned with the expected goals of K-12 education. This infrastructure would integrate and foster collaboration and innovation among teacher preparation institutions, districts, teacher organizations, and other providers of professional development.

- Develop formal pathways for teachers to advance in their profession, which may include but not require entering administration for advancement.

IMPLICATIONS FOR STATE AND DISTRICT LEADERS, DEPARTMENT OF ELEMENTARY AND SECONDARY EDUCATION LEADERS, AND SUPERINTENDENTS

Clear and bold vision

- Develop and execute a communications strategy that conveys the goals of the system to relevant stakeholders, translates those into specific learning goals and curriculum, and highlights good practice at the classroom and school level in supporting instruction aligned with those goals, as well as practices at the district level that are supportive of such instruction. Contribute to building a positive narrative about public education that showcases positive examples of practice, and that values expert knowledge developed by practitioners. As part of this strategy, support the creation of a platform that supports the sharing and use of knowledge developed by practitioners about effective 21st century education practices.

- Strengthen articulation between districts and teacher education institutions in ways that provide continuous training and support for district administrators and principals in conducting meaningful evaluations and identifying actionable recommendations for improving classroom practice.

- Develop the capacity of school boards to create leadership pipelines that encourage growth from teacher to principal to superintendent within the systems so that the values of the school system are sustained long-term.

Commitment to implementation

- Create incentives for collaboration between districts to allow them to more cost effectively differentiate how the diverse needs of students are serviced. This might ultimately lead to more district consolidation to increase program options, reduce administrative overhead, and increase direct support to students.

Coherence

- Define and clarify roles within the system in ways that bring different efforts and initiatives for achieving education goals into alignment.

- Develop multiple and fluid relationships between various institutions in the system to strengthen connections between policy and practice. This might include a Department of Elementary and Secondary Education (DESE) program that provides several teacher and principal residencies, and more field visits by DESE staff.
    - Teachers and Principals would serve one to two year residencies at DESE to better inform the development of new policies and regulations from a practitioner's perspective.
    - DESE staff would spend more time in the field observing and seeking input from practitioners regarding how DESE can best support practitioners in the field.

Capacity

- Advance initiatives that support the creation of school cultures anchored in the recognition of education as an expert profession, and that cultivate and reward expertise and professional merit.

- Develop teacher career ladders with multiple and ongoing opportunities for professional development aligned with expected goals. Include opportunities for rotations into multiple roles at various levels of the system in teacher trajectories as a way to create shared perspective and stronger inputs into policy making and teacher training.

- Advance substantial initiatives to support ongoing professional development of teachers in ways that leverage public-private partnerships to foster innovation, effectiveness, and impact at scale.

- Establish high quality mentor program for all new principals, just as there are for superintendents and teachers.

IMPLICATIONS FOR TEACHER EDUCATION INSTITUTIONS, DEPARTMENT OF HIGHER EDUCATION AND PRESIDENTS/ EDUCATION PROGRAM LEADERS

Coherence

- Participate in collaboratives of institutions that seek to align teacher preparation program goals with system level goals.

- Strengthen curriculum of teacher preparation to better support the development of capacities to teach competencies necessary for life in the 21st century (cognitive, intrapersonal and interpersonal).

Capacity

- Raise entry and exit requirements for candidates into teacher preparation programs so graduates have the necessary capacities for effective and powerful instruction. For example, for undergraduate teacher education programs these should include:

- Solid academic preparation at the pre-collegiate level.
- Letters of recommendation from current teachers specifically indicating a candidate's potential as a teacher.
- Stronger practice-based residency experiences early in and throughout the teacher preparation program.
- Completion of a performance-based assessment under supervision of an accomplished teacher and preparation program supervisor before becoming a teacher of record.

- Establish robust feedback loops with schools and districts that place graduates so as to continuously improve teacher preparation to serve the requirements of students in those schools. Once teachers enter the work force, there should be a strong connection between districts and teacher education institutions to provide feedback on teacher preparedness, to better inform and improve teacher preparation programs, and to provide additional job embedded supports and professional development.

- Create incentives for faculty to engage with practitioners in school improvement efforts and to collaborate with practitioners in codifying knowledge generated by expert practitioners.

- Improve the selection criteria of mentor teachers to ensure the best possible role models for new teachers. Require a rotation within internship placements to allow exposure to a broad swath of pedagogy and student populations.

IMPLICATIONS FOR SCHOOL LEADERS

Clear and bold vision

- Create school cultures anchored in the recognition of education as an expert profession, that cultivate and reward expertise and professional merit, and that are built on the belief that "we can't afford to waste any talent."

Capacity

- Create opportunities for job-embedded continuous teacher development. Build partnerships with other schools and teacher preparation institutions for this purpose.

- Develop talent management systems built on the premise that we can't afford to waste any talent.

- Develop school cultures that foster collaboration and teamwork in achieving results for students.

- Foster cultures open to continuous learning and improvement, including learning from other schools and school systems.

- Emphasize effective teaching practice and differentiated support for students rather than class size and other statistically less significant drivers of student growth.

IMPLICATIONS FOR TEACHERS

Clear and bold vision

- Identify the curriculum goals and to translate those into effective curriculum and pedagogies.

Capacity

- Develop the necessary expertise to support effective instructional practice and become professionals who are continuously learning.

- Codify their own practice in ways that adds to the knowledge base about powerful instruction and 21st century education.

- Place a premium on collaboration and continuous learning from peers.

Implications for the Public

Clear and bold vision

- Develop and implement programs so that the public will see teachers as nation builders who are developing the talent of all young people by preparing them for success in a 21st century knowledge economy and as active participants in our democratic institutions.

Commitment to implementation

- Hold elected officials accountable for providing the necessary support to public schools so they can meet the learning needs of students in the 21st century. Support education as a high priority policy of elected officials with adequate budgets, skilled leadership, and the sustained effort necessary to allow policy cycles to yield results and to support ongoing learning and improvement.

Capacity

- Provide resources to educate school committee members on the fundamental drivers for effective education so they can support and promote them within their district.

Letter 1. Lessons for improving the quality of teacher preparation programs and instruction in the commonwealth

— By Paul F. Toner
President, Cambridge Strategic Partnerships
Member, Massachusetts Board of Higher
Education

The origins of the visit to Singapore – The Singaporean context –
Factors contributing to educational success –
Centralized versus decentralized –
Teachers as nation builders – Connection
between policy, practice and research –
Career ladders and leadership programs

In late September, 2014, I had the opportunity to attend a gathering at the Harvard Graduate School of Education hosted by Professor Fernando Reimers. The reason for the gathering was to meet and hear from a delegation of education leaders from the Singaporean Ministry of Education and National Institute of Education (NIE). Professor Reimers' research on global education policies and systems identified Singapore as being at the top of the list of nations improving educational outcomes for all of its children. Professor Reimers had invited a variety of Massachusetts education policymakers and practitioners, including the Commissioner of Education, numerous urban superintendents, teacher preparation faculty from public and private higher education, and other parties interested in learning some lessons for improving the quality of our own teacher preparation programs and the quality of instruction in our commonwealth. As a result of this initial meeting, Professor Reimers and I set about coordinating a tour of Singapore for Massachusetts policymakers, academics, and practitioners from October 9 to 16, 2015. The purpose of the trip was to learn more about the teacher preparation and principal leadership programs that they have put in place, and to determine if there are lessons that can be implemented in Massachusetts.

Singapore is a small nation with a population similar in size to that of Massachusetts and with a geographical area approximately the size of New York City. Both Singapore and Massachusetts score well on international benchmarks of academic achievement, and both are knowledge-based economies where their most valuable resource is the development of the potential of each of their citizens. Although very different in terms of history, governance, and culture, Singapore has some lessons for Massachusetts in the areas of educator and leadership preparation and development.

Singapore celebrated its 50th anniversary as a nation in 2015. In its very short history, Singapore has had four major education transformations and has experienced rapid change in both its education system and economy. It has transitioned from an education system focused simply on universal literacy and primary education, to one that aims for universal high school graduation and post-secondary success. It has transitioned from a low-skill, low-pay third world nation in 1965, to a first world economy today. Singapore is now the 3rd richest country as measured by per capita gross domestic product (GDP). Its economic success is credited to the emphasis on education. Moreover, in Singapore, education and the economy are intertwined. The economic imperative for this emphasis is clear—it is essential to their survival as a nation, and this imperative is accepted by all. As a result, Singapore is now moving forward again in transitioning to a system that emphasizes 21st century skills and values-driven student-centered education.

Singapore is very explicit about its goals of educating every child to his or her fullest potential and developing the nation's human capital system. With a 0.08% birth rate and a 1% unemployment rate, Singapore can't afford to have any of its children fail. Singapore's population includes a multiracial permanent resident population composed of Chinese, Malay and Indian but is also heavily reliant on the immigration of foreign workers and this reliance is trending upwards to aid in compensating for the low birth rate. It was evident during our visit that there is a real meritocracy and a value placed on ensuring that every individual play a valuable role in society. There is individual choice regarding what field of study or work to enter into, but the system does rely heavily on testing and tracking at the end of primary school to guide students into college or career tracks. In Singapore, the students are made accountable for their own learning at a very early age, and families are heavily invested in their children's success. 90% of kids participate in out-of-school test preparation to help prepare them for the Primary School Leaving Examination (PSLE). On our visit we were told that approximately 3% of GDP is spent on test preparation. The curriculum emphasizes math literacy and building student attention span, which differs significantly from language based literacy that is emphasized in curricula in American schools. All of these factors and components have put Singaporean students at the top of global rankings such as the Programme for International Student Assessment (PISA) and other international benchmarks.

The system is focused on developing students to play a productive role in society. This is accepted by the citizenry based on their Confucian belief system which emphasizes setting the needs of the collective society above those of the individual. There is, however, growing concern of income inequality and evidence that what was once believed to be a pure meritocracy is becoming a "hereditary meritocracy" where well-educated and high-income Singaporeans are able to give their children a substantial advantage.

The big issues that Singapore is struggling with are similar to those in Massachusetts. Both espouse the goals of educating all children to the fullest of their abilities and potential, and of providing everyone a meaningful place in their economy going forward. At the same time, both also acknowledge the need to educate the whole child and the need for the development of 21st century skills in students. From what I observed in Singapore, the lessons for Massachusetts are the following:

1. Centralized versus Decentralized

The Singaporean Ministry of Education and NIE have an uncanny ability to look forward to where they need to be five to ten years down the road, and they are exceptional at developing and implementing their plans for getting there. There is a very close link between their educational system and the job market. The system is nimble and swift in making changes. Education leaders are able to accomplish this through a combination of centralization and decentralization. They are centralized in terms of economies of scale, efficiencies of system, and tactical empowerment. They don't have a law called No Child Left Behind, but they have so few children they can't afford any mistakes. The Singaporean education system has strong strategic alignment. They are decentralized in that they provide school leaders and educators with tactical empowerment. They are clear about goals and standards, but school-level leadership decides how to meet them. They believe in being highly accountable and responsible. Schools and educators are very responsive to the external accountability system, but are also able to exercise to their professional judgment at the local level For Singaporean educators, being accountable is being responsible, and being responsible is being accountable.

2. Teachers as Nation Builders

Teachers and principals are respected and heralded publicly as nation builders. The Ministry of Education and National Institute of Education are the policy enablers that support this vision. They identify, recruit, train, and prepare teachers to serve in the 350 schools throughout the nation. Schools and students must meet a very high level for proficiency. No matter what school you go to, you are guaranteed an excellent education. As they say in Singapore, "All schools are good schools."

In addition, the NIE serves as the only preparation and accreditation program for teachers and principals. This reliance on a single institution has its pros and cons, but it is the most significant structural difference between the Massachusetts system, which has approximately 80 separate teacher preparation programs and a separate Department of Education which accredits programs and provides teacher licensure and certifications.

3. Connection between Policy, Practice and Research

The NIE does much more than prepare and accredit teachers and principals; the NIE is held accountable by the government and profession by having to answer the question "What value are you adding to the profession, to practice, to supporting schools and ultimately the growth of the nation?" Thus, the NIE must demonstrate its relevance to schools continuously. It must be responsive to the needs of practitioners, provide support, and coordinate resources.

The NIE is also the source of knowledge and skill development through its generating of content and pedagogy. It is responsible for creating and fostering partnerships among practitioners, policy makers, government, and business. Ministry and NIE staff frequently visits schools. Teachers and principals are regularly cycling through the NIE as part of their career development. The NIE is staffed with many practitioners who bring alignment between well-intentioned policy and real classroom practice. The NIE has also been involved in educational research, along with the government. However, the government's investment in research is limited by resource constraints, and focuses on that which is pragmatic and useful to classroom educators. Therefore, research is focused on pedagogy and practice, as opposed to social justice issues.

4. Career Ladders and Leadership Programs

The NIE has a career map that spans from novice to career to master teacher. It recruits and trains new teachers from the top students in the country, and provides them with the highest, most rigorous academic training that will prepare them for any profession—not only for life as a teacher in the classroom. Master's degree candidates have a very clear focus on what they would like to study and work on. Training and preparation does not end with entrance into the profession; it occurs throughout their career.

The NIE has developed clearly defined leadership programs for developing principals, teacher leaders, administrators, and curriculum specialists. These programs are not self-selected; through continuous evaluation, supervision, and feedback during their careers in the classroom, educators, along with their principals, identify their strengths and interests in order to build a career path and to provide them with the training they need for the next stage of their career. The Leadership Program offered by the NIE involves exposure to international education experiences, visiting businesses and industries, and discussions with senior Ministry and NIE leaders. This all contributes to educators thinking out of the box, seeing connections, and developing a vision for the future of education and the nation.

The Career Action Project is the capstone of the principal training process. Principals-in-training are assigned to a project outside of their comfort zone. They participate in an exercise that requires them to envision the needs of society five, ten, and fifteen years down the road. They then need to think about what schools need to do to prepare students for this future reality. All the while, they have no institutional authority to implement their ideas. They are "nobody" in their assigned schools. Therefore, they have to develop a plan to lead by persuasion, by influence. This exercise stretches them as leaders. They must learn to work well with others, collaborate, and innovate in order to move things forward. And, as a quality control, the current school principals, who have been through the same program, are the gatekeepers in the schools regarding any further implementation.

5. Continuous Improvement and Innovation

As a society and education system, Singapore is focused on continuous improvement. Although it is at the top of international rankings such as PISA, the country's leaders recognize that the educational system that they have built is not sufficient for the success of their students and their society going forward. They have created a system that is heavily reliant on academics and test scores, which has served them well, but they know that moving forward they must infuse 21st century skills and habits of learning in the teachers and students to prepare their society to maintain relevance in an ever changing global economy. To do this, they have invited American universities and other institutions from the United States and Europe to help them develop a more student-centered model of education. They are also moving toward a values-based education system and are asking education leaders the question, "What does it mean to be a citizen of Singapore?" They are conscious of the fact that in the new global economy they must be constantly reflecting and reimagining their role in the world. They have served as a hub of finance and manufacturing for large global corporations, but they are now asking how do they produce their own inventors and innovators? They seek to build a system that will produce Singapore's future Mark Zuckerberg, Bill Gates, and Steve Jobs.

In conclusion, I believe there are a number of lessons that Massachusetts can learn from Singapore in the areas of teacher and principal leadership development. Although our systems vary greatly in many respects, the success of the Singapore education system is based on a focused strategic alignment of resources around a common vision and a belief that schools and educators are the key to the success of the nation. In Singapore, they believe that they cannot afford to lose one child in the process – neither can we – and through strong leadership at the state level, Massachusetts can build a similarly successful system of teacher and principal leadership programs.

Letter 2. Sharing the Singapore Story: Reflections on the Visit by U.S. Education Leaders

— By Oon-Seng Tan, PhD
Director, National Institute of Education,
Singapore

Hosting two delegations – NIE's key roles –
NIE's strategic roadmap: Building our knowledge capital by 2017 –
Developing star programmes – Strengthening 21st century pedagogies –
Impacting the education fraternity through educational research –
Enhancing Partnerships with Stakeholders

On the 12th and 13th of October, 2015, the National Institute of Education (NIE) was proud to play host to two groups of education leaders from the United States. The first group comprised educators and education leaders based in Texas, and was led by Colorado State Senator, Mike Johnston, who represents Denver. This group was keen to learn more about the professional development and training of school leaders. The other delegation were education leaders from Massachusetts, led by Paul Toner, the president of Cambridge Strategic Partnerships and former president of the Massachusetts Teachers Association, and Professor Fernando Reimers, the NIE's 2015 C.J. Koh Professor and the Harvard Graduate School of Education's Ford Foundation Professor of Practice in International Education. This second group was interested in learning more about Singapore's education system as a whole.

I was heartened and honored to share Singapore's system-wide education story and cherished the opportunity to meet like-minded educators from across the globe—those who share the same vision and passion about the importance of education. I had the opportunity to formally address both groups and to provide an overview of the NIE which prepares all teachers for Singapore's schools, and to share our vision, mission, key roles, and strategic directions. I will attempt to summarise what I spoke about so that delegates can look at this document and recall key learning points.

NIE's Key Roles

Today, Singapore's National Institute of Education is rated the tenth institution of higher education in the field of education according to the 2015 Quacquarelli Symonds (QS) World University rankings. NIE aims to be a world-class institute of distinction renowned for excellence in teacher education and education research. As the only teacher accreditation institute in Singapore, NIE works closely with the Ministry of Education in fulfilling its four key roles:

1. Preparing the next generation of teachers through initial teacher preparation programmes.

2. Upgrading the quality of the teaching force and developing world-class school leaders through responsive professional development programmes.

3. Conducting education research to develop innovative pedagogies to transform teaching and learning in schools and in our own programmes, thus keeping Singapore in the forefront of global education systems.

4. Providing consultancy services to export the NIE brand of teacher education globally.

NIE's Strategic Roadmap: Building Our Knowledge Capital by 2017

When I took over as NIE's Director in July 2014, I worked with my senior management team to come up with a new strategic roadmap that will move us towards 2017. A key goal component of this strategy involves building our knowledge capital through the development of star programmes, strengthening our 21st century pedagogies, and enhancing our research capabilities.

1. Developing Star Programmes

Our initial teacher education, higher degree, and professional development courses are designed to provide a holistic teacher education experience. This involves educating the whole person through a multidisciplinary approach, providing depth of disciplinary and pedagogical content knowledge. This is done through research and evidence-informed programme development, through offering global perspectives through international exposure, and through strong partnerships with schools and industries with an emphasis on a values-based philosophy for character development.

Our premier scholars' programme, the Nanyang Technical University (NTU)-NIE Teaching Scholar Programme (TSP), was launched in 2014. The NTU-NIE TSP is a programme of strategic significance for the NIE and the Singaporean education system. With the long-term aim of raising the standard of the teaching profession in Singapore, the TSP signals a major shift towards quality, rather than quantity, in teacher recruitment and development.

Following almost two years of development in close collaboration with MOE and NTU, the enhanced four-year Bachelor of Arts/Bachelor of Science (in Education) programmes will offer a robust curriculum, allowing student teachers to deepen their content and pedagogical mastery. There will be opportunities for student teachers to undertake both content and education research, and to participate in international conferences, overseas practicum stints, and semester-abroad exchange programmes.

Beyond the bachelor programmes, the Postgraduate Diploma in Education (PGDE) programme will also see significant enhancement. It will be lengthened from the current 12 months to 16 months—starting with the December 2016 cohort. The extension of the PGDE programme will allow student teachers the time and space to deepen their sense of professional ethos, strengthen their pedagogical content knowledge, and to better their practice. These elements are critical for providing teachers with a strong grounding for adaptive capabilities in response to the ever-evolving educational landscape.

The NIE is also proud to partner with top international education institutions to offer joint masters programmes. The Master of Arts in Leadership and Educational Change (MALEC) is jointly developed and taught by faculty from NIE and Teachers College, Columbia University.

Furthermore, the NIE's flagship leadership programmes are widely recognized as being multi-disciplinary and future-oriented. They aim to provide school leaders a developmental platform to reflect on their beliefs as educators and future school leaders. Through a transformational mindset philosophy, leaders will discover that they are in the position to lead, care, and inspire teachers and students. Delegates were also able to meet with the Management and School Leadership (MLS) participants who showcased their experiences and reflections on their recent trips to other countries in the region at the MLS "Gallery Walk." Such trips provide not just international exposure to future school leaders, but also the challenge to reflect on both on the traditional ways things are done in Singaporean schools as compared to how these are handled differently overseas.

2. Strengthening 21st Century Pedagogies

The NIE has established an institute-wide teaching and learning framework aimed at providing a learner-centric "21st century learning experience," which will encompass the elements of experiential, participative, inquiry-based, inter-connected, and collaborative learning. We will be embarking our curriculum design to incorporate the latest information and communication technology (ICT) and pedagogical innovations to meet the needs of a new generation of learners. Under this new framework, teaching and learning will take on a borderless, seamless, personalised, multi-modal, anytime-and-anywhere approach.

Currently, our lecture theatres are being transformed to become collaborative learning spaces.

3. Impacting the Education Fraternity Through Educational Research

Our Office of Education Research oversees the development, dissemination, and administration of the education research of the NIE. We see ourselves as holding a very unique position by serving the needs of both our parent university, NTU, and our education system through preparing teachers for our schools. As an institute within the university, it is of vital importance to continue to invest in and enhance our research capabilities. In serving our role as the national teacher education institution, our researchers work closely with schools and communities to bring about evidence-based and research-informed pedagogical improvements. In the process, these enhancements improve teaching competencies systemically and keep Singapore at the forefront of global education systems.

4. Enhancing Partnerships with Stakeholders

The NIE has formed very strong partnerships with Ministry of Education academies, in particular the Academy of Singapore Teachers (AST). Our collaborations with the AST help us to develop and deliver more relevant and up-to-date teacher education, leadership, professional development, and research intervention programmes. NIE is partnering with the AST and MOE to implement a new model of teacher training and development, called "Authentic Onsite Professional Development," at the Centre for Teaching and Learning Excellence at Yusof Ishak Secondary School.

The NIE has also moved towards school-based workshops run specifically for a school or a school cluster. This is an important area of professioanl develpment work that we would like to see continue and therefore we encourage faculty to be more pro-active in being ambassadors of NIE's work.

The NIE is also stepping up efforts to engage schools and school teachers in intervention projects and other research initiatives. We are doing this in a variety of ways—from workshops and situated professional development programmes at the AST and schools, to sharing sessions with school clusters, professional learning communities, and networked learning communities. Through these efforts, the number of school intervention projects has been growing; we are now involved in over 100 projects with schools distributed evenly all over the island.

Strategic partnerships in the areas of student exchange and research collaborations will continue to be strengthened and built with top institutes of higher learning. These partners include Harvard University, Stanford University, Cambridge University, University College London, Boston College, and Teachers College, Columbia University. Additionally, we have signed and renewed our strategic agreements with: Stockholm University, Sweden; University College London's Institute of Education, UK; Korea National Sport University, South Korea; and University of Helsinki, Finland.

In all of the key roles and strategic directions taken by NIE, there is systemic coherence between key educational stakeholders—namely, the Ministry of Education, the schools, and the NIE. This ensures that as a system, we have goal congruence and alignment, and seriousness of purpose and intent in turning these goals into reality system-wide.

Sharing the Singapore story tells only one side of what transpired during the visit. For me, the richness of the conversations, the depth of the questions asked and the sincerity in wanting to learn from another system touched me most about this group of American education leaders. I am convinced that with top education leaders from the United States adopting such a learning, inquiring mindset, can only augur well for the future of education in the United States—ensuring, truly, that no child will be left behind in the race to the top.

LETTER 3. PLANNING THE VISIT BY U.S. EDUCATION LEADERS: FROM CONCEPTUALISATION TO REALISATION

— By Ee-Ling Low, PhD

Head of Strategic Planning and Academic
Quality, National Institute of Education,
Singapore

*Preamble — Planning the programme —
Building and sustaining a high quality teaching
workforce: The Singapore Story —
Demonstrating passion and commitment
towards learning from other systems*

Preamble

Sometime in January 2015, Fernando Reimers, the National Institute of Education's (NIE) 2015 C.J. Koh Professor and Harvard Graduate School of Education's Ford Foundation Professor of Practice in International Education approached our director, Professor Tan Oon-Seng, about the possibility of hosting a group of education leaders from Massachusetts who are interested in learning more about the Singaporean education system. He readily agreed and warmly welcomed the idea as well as the prospect of hosting this group of visitors. By the middle of the year, we also received a request from Colorado State Senator Mike Johnston who was keen to lead another team of educators and leaders from Texas to learn about school leadership preparation in Singapore. We therefore decided to invite both visiting delegations to come at the same time and were determined to customize the visit to ensure that both teams fulfilled their trip objectives.

Planning the Programme

Shortly before the visit was to take place, Professor Reimers narrowed the focus of the trip and offered an idea of what the programme might look like with input from key members of the visiting delegations. The programme included a thorough introduction to the key role of the

National Institute of Education in Singapore, and how it fits within the education system, as well as a general introduction to the Singaporean education at the outset of the visit. Meetings and presentations were planned so as to learn about what Singapore does to support new teachers, the nature and structure of mentoring for these teachers, and how the schools work together with the Ministry of Education to ensure a smooth transition into the teaching workforce. Additionally, delegates were interested in the bigger picture of how teachers are selected, recruited, and prepared—both in initial teacher education and ongoing professional development throughout their careers. The careful selection and intentional preparation of school leaders for Singapore was also a focal area for both groups. Finally, Professor Reimers suggested visits to the Institute of Technical Education (ITE) and several schools that he had been impressed with during his maiden visit to Singapore in 2014.

With these clear objectives in mind, the challenge was to squeeze this wish list into three working days[13]—which we did! The final programme included an opening address by NIE Director, Professor Tan Oon-Seng, on NIE's key roles; an introduction and sharing session on the Singapore education system; a session on school leadership development in Singapore; NIE's milestone leadership programmes presentations on both initial teacher education and professional development programmes by the Offices of Teacher Education (OTE) and Graduate Studies and Professional Learning (GPL), respectively; and a presentation/roundtable discussion with principals and teacher development leaders at the Academy of Singapore Teachers (AST). Additionally, site visits were organized to the Institute of Technical Education Central campus, an elementary school (Nan Chiau Primary) and a secondary school (Crescent Girls School).

The next part of my reflections include the main points from my session with the delegates on "Building and Sustaining a High Quality Teaching Workforce: The Singapore Story."

---

[13] While the delegations were in Singapore for more than three days, the NIE was only involved in planning programming for three of those days.

Letter 3

Building and Sustaining a High Quality Teaching Workforce: The Singapore Story

I began my presentation by asking the question, "How does Singapore ensure and sustain and high quality teaching workforce?" I began by talking about recruitment and selection—how teachers are selected from the top one-third of each cohort (as that is the percentage that qualify for higher education each year) and how only one in eight candidates, on average, are successful after an interview and selection process that screens for aptitude, positive attitudes, and personality attributes suitable for teaching. Each year, about 200-300 teaching scholarships are given by the Ministry of Education, which can be used either locally or abroad.

The next point I raised was about the high regard that the Singaporean society has for the teaching profession. From the moment Singapore gained independence as a nation in 1965, the role of teachers has been tied integrally to the important mission of nation building. Until recently, billboards displayed at the back of buses by the Ministry of Education depicted powerful slogans reminding us that this message has remained consistent throughout the past 50 years: "Teachers... shaping the future of our nation, one student at a time." I have seen this strong messaging in only one other system I have visited—in Finland.

Once candidates are selected for pre-service teacher education, tuition fees are paid for by the Ministry of Education and, on top of this, student teachers are also given a monthly stipend. The starting salaries of teachers are competitive and matched against beginning accountants and engineers in the civil service.

Singapore's leadership also believe in a highly rigorous pre-service teacher education programme that is underpinned by a values-driven paradigm with a three-pronged set of principles that serve as the pillar of our teacher education model. These are: learner-centredness, strong sense of teacher identity, and service to the profession and the community. In my presentation, I also highlighted key components of our pre-service teacher education programmes that aim to develop graduates who are shapers of character, facilitators of learning, architects of learning environments, and leaders of educational change. As the delegates were going to be briefed by the Office of Teacher Education, I did not elaborate further on our pre-service programmes except to mention that creating a close theory-practice nexus was a top priority, and we do this by ensuring there were maximal opportunities for reflection—not least via the electronic teaching and learning portfolio—and ensuring that there were several clinical practice postings, each carefully structured and with appropriate mentors.

Equally importantly is how we track the quality of the programmes we deliver. This is done via surveys administered at different points in time and to different audiences. The end-of-programme evaluation survey is administered to all student teachers across all intakes and programmes. The Graduate Preparedness Survey (GPS) is administered to beginning teachers to ask them for their thoughts about how well they feel they have been prepared one to two years after their graduation. The Stakeholders Survey (SS) is distributed to school leaders and senior personnel with the responsibility of overseeing the beginning teachers so they have a chance to provide feedback about the quality of our programmes. Additionally, intake profile trends and graduation results are also tracked for each cohort. Collectively, the trend data and survey results are used to provide an evidence base from which to inform the future development and enhancement of our programmes.

Teacher professional growth and development is also not left to chance and is part of the vision to develop an educator who is ethical, a competent professional, a collaborative learner, a transformational leader, and a community builder as articulated in Singapore's teacher growth model. Further, career progression is mapped out along three tracks: teaching, leadership, and specialist according to the teachers' talents and aspirations.

Finally, I concluded my presentation by distilling the Singapore education journey along six main points: selecting and attracting top quality educators, providing them with competitive compensation and salary packages, the professionalization of the teaching profession, careful and intentional school leadership development, systemic coherence, and an emphasis on always learning from other systems.

Demonstrating Passion and Commitment Towards Learning from Other Systems

I end this reflection by sharing how impressed I was personally by the genuine spirit of learning displayed by the delegates. They demonstrated unrivalled passion and deep commitment towards learning from other education systems. This made all of us who had the privilege of mingling with the delegates experience a truly enriching and intellectual journey of professional exchange. We were inspired by the questions and the seriousness that the delegates put into their efforts to understand more about Singapore's education system. The quality of the professional conversations and exchanges that took place in all the meetings made me grateful to be part of this learning journey with my American colleagues. I only hope that they found the long journey here worthwhile, and I look forward to continued collaborations and burgeoning professional partnerships in the future.

Letter 4. Reflections on a Nation by a New Hampshire Teacher of the Year

— By Joey Lee
Education Programs Manager,
Education First

The importance of reflection – Ethnic harmony through policy –
Systemic coherence of education and economic need –
Lessons learned and questions that remain

While travelling in Thailand in July of 2014, my wife and I met a Buddhist monk who inspired us by sharing his thought that living without reflecting is like eating without digesting—a logical and powerful metaphor. I have referenced this phrase many times since returning, both internally and externally. I have asked my students in the classroom to reflect on the phrase, to digest its meaning, to apply this reflective practice to their learning process. I have asked the student athletes I had coached to make meaning of the phrase, to apply it to athletics and adversity. I have asked myself if I practice what I ask of others, if I take appropriate time to make meaning of new experiences. In October of 2015, I was fortunate to join a delegation of educators from Massachusetts to travel to Singapore and explore how this nation attracts, certifies, and retains quality educators. As I reflect, I am validated in my thought that it is essential to understand a nation and its origins before attempting to understand how they choose to educate their youth.

Singapore, an island city-state celebrating its golden jubilee, is a nation rooted in cultural tradition and which prides itself on strategic planning in order to remain an economic epicenter, while also establishing cohesion as one nation with a clear vision for the future. This balance of tradition and progress—of past and future—is equally evident in Singapore's education system. World-renowned for their recent and continuous success on OECD's Program for International Student Assessment (PISA), Singapore has drawn the interest of educators from around the world. It is clear that Singaporeans have chosen to invest in their people and to place high value on their education. As this small island nation has limited other natural resources, its people are its future.

Ethnic Harmony Through Policy

Situated geographically within a triangle made up of the world's most populated nations, China, India, and Indonesia, Singapore is a nation that has achieved cultural harmony and prosperity through strict adherence to government policy. This is likely the result of influential events that took place just prior to independence: race riots between ethnic Chinese and Malay in the early 1960s played a role in Singapore's expulsion from Malaysia. Lee Kwan Yew, Singapore's founding father and first Prime Minister, recognized the importance of ensuring peace between the people of the new nation. Thus, in order to promote social cohesion, the government instituted policies of immersion rather than segregation. For example, all public housing (in which roughly 85% of all Singaporeans reside) have an ethnic quota that must reflect the ethnic mix of the nation. Citizens are raised to accept cultural differences and to live within close proximity to those who hold different beliefs. There is very little questioning of this and other policies, since citizens seem to accept authoritarian rule more easily than would citizens of a traditional western nation, who are perhaps more likely to protest in the name of personal freedoms. Singaporeans seemed to believe that the decisions made by their policymakers are in the best interest of the people of the nation. In essence, governance makes policy to support the collective rather than individuals, since there is a sense that the whole is better than the sum of its parts.

Systemic Coherence of Education and Economic Need

Singaporeans divide their educational history into four eras, with the current described as student-centered and values driven. The Ministry of Education has developed this strategy with the intent of producing citizens that are confident and concerned, who are active contributors, and who are self-driven learners. They hope to produce a globally-relevant but locally-rooted citizenship, which is a challenge in what Sing Kong Lee, former director of the National Institute of Education (NIE), describes as a "volatile, uncertain, complex, and ambiguous" knowledge-based globalized world. To maximize efficiency, Singapore assesses their youth in the 6th grade with a high stakes standardized test, the Primary School Leaving Exam (PSLE). The results of this exam determine one of three paths that a student will take for secondary school. While each path focuses on academic pursuits, those who test poorly attend to the Institute of Technical Education (ITE) where students focus on preparation for employability and lifelong learning rather than pursuit of an academic university degree. ITE schools educate for workforce readiness, which contributed to low unemployment, hovering around 2% for the past 30 years, and contributing to an already strong economy.

This synergistic relationship between education and the workforce is led by strong leadership and coherence between educators at all levels of the system. All teachers and principals are certified by just one organization, the NIE, where each candidate must complete a research project in order to earn their degree. Teaching is a highly competitive field, and as a result teachers are compensated with salaries equivalent to that of an engineer. The NIE is also the only institution that certifies principals. Each principal candidate must complete a Creative Action Project (CAP) where they are paired with a school district and mentor principal. The candidate uses the school as a case study, exploring policies and practice, and must hypothesize what the school's needs might be in 10-15 years. Furthermore, the candidate must make suggestions to the principal regarding at least one immediate change that should be made in order to improve the school, and then must convince the principal to actually make that change. This allows the mentor principal to be the first gatekeeper, and once the plan is approved, the candidate must implement that change including by convincing the fellow administrators, teachers, and community members that the change is in the best interest of all involved. This refines the candidate's ability to lead by influence, since they have no position of official authority or clout to rely upon when making that change.

Lessons Learned and Questions that Remain

The Singaporean education system and form of governance has produced an economic and educational success story, but one might argue whether the success comes at the cost of individual autonomy and freedom of expression. There was concern raised by certain Singaporean educators that there is far too much stress on both educators and students alike in a system that is so reliant on high stakes testing—which proves that some issues in education truly defy borders, since we hear this complaint often in the United States. In addition, in the current digital age, now that parents have a more transparent view of their child's education, some teachers worried that they can no longer just teach students, but must also regularly answer to those who might have a narrow view of the classroom's needs. Of course, there are characteristics which are desirable within the Singaporean education system that can be transferred home to one district or one state, but would be a challenge to scale nationwide. Regardless, as noted in the sections above, there are lessons to be learned from the Singaporean system and I find myself grateful for the opportunity to explore a new country, and am rejuvenated by the resounding passion of my fellow travelers.

LETTER 5. TEACHERS AND TEACHER EDUCATION IN SINGAPORE

— BY ELEONORA VILLEGAS-REIMERS, EdD
Chair of the Department of Elementary and
Special Education, Wheelock College

*A learning experience – Twelve consistent messages –
Two topics curiously absent – The role of early childhood education –
Addressing students with special needs*

I had the opportunity to be part of a delegation of American educators from Massachusetts who spent five full days in October 2015 learning about teachers and teacher education in Singapore. This was my second visit to the country; my first visit had been two and half years before for a week to teach a graduate level course on child and adolescent development to early childhood educators in Singapore who were starting a master's degree program with my home institution, Wheelock College. At that time, I was the teacher who came prepared with a syllabus, readings, assignments, class activities, case studies, videos, and endless questions that helped students learn about child development while I learned about the Singaporean contexts where the children these teachers were working with were developing and learning. This time, however, I was the student who was eager, ready to learn, to listen, to ask, to question, and to come back from this weeklong experience to reflect on teacher education in Singapore and the United States.

Thinking back to these very productive five days in October, I see that there were several themes and messages that we all received consistently from everyone we met and listened to. Indeed, it was the consistency that caught the attention of many of us in the delegation, as there appeared to be complete agreement across institutions, individuals, policies, and practices. There were also two missing themes that I found myself asking about consistently during the week, only to find that the answers were not as consistent or as clear as all others. First, let me comment on the consistent, explicit messages, and then reflect on the two very important missing pieces.

Everywhere we visited and everyone who spoke with us (including teachers and administrators in a high school for girls, an elementary school, and a technical high school; faculty, students and administrators from the National Institute of Education; members of the teacher's union; and several organizations that support teacher professional development) shared the following messages with us, consistently:

1. **Teachers are professionals.** As such they are selected, prepared, educated, paid, and treated by society.

2. **Selection into the teaching profession is key.** Admission into teacher preparation programs is highly competitive. Being highly selective appears to be one of the elements that has made teaching such a valued profession, and, according to the educators we met, one of the factors that explains the recent success of the education system in Singapore.

3. **There is a very clear and well-known structure of the education system in Singapore.** It did not matter how the system was graphed, drawn, or described in words, the specific structure of the system was presented the same way by all people we listened to. Everyone described the structure, the system, and the relationships between and among the different elements of the system in the same way. There is a clear sense of responsibility built into each of the elements of the system, and a clear function for each. There is also a clear sense of how each individual moves through the different elements of the system, whether he or she is a student or a professional educator who has a clear sense of his or her career path and options from the start.

4. **There is a very clear understanding by all of the aims of education in Singapore.** The country is unified behind the goals of education, and thus there is a clear, unified vision of the purposes of teacher education programs as well. Nation building is the key goal

at the present, and everyone seems to support those aims completely, despite the fact that top officials in the Ministry of Education select the aims.

5. **Assessment is key throughout the system and strong performance is expected and supported.** High expectations at all levels are the norm. Teacher candidates are assessed regularly as they go through a teacher preparation program. Professional teachers are assessed regularly, and major career advancement decisions are made based on the results of those assessments, from movement through the system to recommending whether the teacher stays in the classroom-pathway, the administrator-pathway, or the high-level-administrator-pathway (where he or she would eventually work at the Ministry of Education).

Assessment is also key in supporting student learning. Students are assessed regularly, in ways that are foreign to American educators. For example, we heard of second graders sitting through hour-and-a-half exams regularly. When asked about whether that was developmentally appropriate for young children whose attention span is not typically believed to be as long as 90 minutes for a test, we were told that making them sit through such a long test is what helps them develop their attention skills.

6. **Student performance at the end of the elementary school years has significant impact on the academic and professional opportunities that student will have for the rest of their lives.** All students in public schools in Singapore take the Primary School Leaving Exam (PSLE—an exam given at the end of the 6th grade). The results of that test determine whether students attend an accelerated high school program, a regular high school program, or a technical high school program. If the technical high school is the only option offered based on the results of the test, the chances that that student will be admitted to a university program are very

small; he or she would have to attend a polytechnic first, and even then there is no guarantee.

7. **The responsibility of students' performance is the students' and their parents'.** It is never, ever, the teachers' responsibility. Whether the students do well or not, the responsibility is always in the hands of the student and his or her parents. The PSLE is so high stakes that many parents take time off from work to help tutor and mentor their children. Parents pay for lots of extra classes, and a substantial amount of time is spent preparing for this life-defining test. Yet, in Singapore, the responsibility of how students perform on this test is never, ever, assigned to the teachers teaching those students.

8. **The content of the elementary education years is quite focused**: Mathematics, Science, English, and mother tongue. Teachers are specialized in one of these four areas as their primary focus during their teacher preparation program. Social Studies, Arts, Health, Socio-emotional learning, etc., are all thought to be important but have no role in the regular curriculum. They are taught as co-curricular subjects in after-school programs. Yet, not all Singapore students participate in school-based after-school programs.

9. **Bilingualism and inter-racial relationships are important, explicitly emphasized and practiced, and are legislated with clear policies.** It is expected that all children in Singapore will be fluent in English since that is the unifying language across racial and ethnic groups; it is expected, also, that each student will be fluent in his or her mother tongue as that preserves each racial/ethnic group that makes up Singapore and shows respect for their culture, including their language. Teachers of all racial and linguistic groups are valued, selected, prepared, and hired in all public schools. Racial and cultural differences are not emphasized or discussed explicitly. When asked, educators we spoke to emphasized the harmony in which the three original ethnic groups live: the Malay, the Chinese

and the Indian. Yet, in very subtle ways, it would appear that some groups do better than others in different tasks, professions, and have different opportunities. This is not discussed openly at all. On one occasion, when asked explicitly about whether there are group differences, one of our presenters said that indeed there was a group that usually performed lower than the other two, and yet never identified that group in any way.

10. **Different levels of education do carry with them different status and level of respect.** Despite major efforts by the country's educators, Singaporean society does attach different statuses to the different kinds of education students receive. Doing poorly on the PSLE and thus being sent to a technical school is still shameful for some families. On the other hand, admission into the best university in the country is a distinction to be celebrated and publicized, and becoming a teacher is a sign of accomplishment.

11. **Teacher unions have a place at the table.** Despite a very centralized system of education where most decisions are made by a few people at the top level of administration, teacher unions are actively engaged in the process of education and teacher preparation, and try to have a voice in high-level decisions. Members of the teacher union were open in discussing their participation in high-level discussions.

12. **International schools are available mostly to foreign students.** Singapore has a number of international schools that welcome children with different levels of ability, linguistic backgrounds, and other differences. These schools are an important part of the education system given the number of foreigners who live and work in Singapore. A very interesting fact about these schools: Singaporeans can only study in those schools if the government gives them special permission to do so. Three reasons qualify students to receive this special permission: the students have studied in another country for a number of years and are now back in Singapore; the

students have a parent who is not Singaporean; and the student has an identified special need.

Each of these twelve messages were explained to us consistently and repeatedly by different people in different institutions throughout the five days of visits and conversations. Every question asked was answered in the same way, with the same emphasis and content, and without a pause or moment to think. That was not the case about two topics that I found curiously absent from the narrative: one was the preparation of special education teachers and the work with children with special learning needs, and the other was early childhood education.

What is the role of early childhood education in the success of the Singaporean system?

It was striking to me how the delegation would be presented with graphs, drawings, and narratives explaining the education system and the education process in Singapore, but early childhood education was not mentioned at all. The education system does not include early childhood; the education process is described as starting in first grade and the preparation of teachers does not include professionals working with children younger than five years old. Why, I wondered? We learned that Singapore offers incentives for families to have more children, and the more children, the larger the incentives. We also learned that policies exist to encourage families to live close together (loans with better terms are given to young families who buy homes near their parents, for example), yet early childhood care and education are thought of as happening outside of the education system. Thus, early childhood teachers are not "teachers," at least not in the way in which they define the professionally prepared, respected, and paid teachers in elementary and secondary education.

At a time when all research shows the importance of stimulation and intentional education in the first five years of life, this top scorer in international tests is not giving the same attention, funding, importance, status, or respect to those who teach the youngest citizens of the country. This is intriguing and something worth studying in much more detail. Confused looks were shared when I asked about early childhood—a quick dismissal of the question, or a not-so-coherent reference to being trained in polytechnic institutes, were the consistent responses I received. Narratives of the Ministry of Education trying to determine where early childhood belongs (whether in the Ministry that oversees the education system or the Ministry that oversees services to families) were shared. I am intrigued by this lack of clarity, especially because of my first experience in Singapore when I taught 38 very intelligent, hard-working, and highly motivated women who work in child care centers, pre-schools, and nursery schools and who are highly qualified and educated. I assume they are not thought of with the same level of professionalism, respect, and admiration that the rest of the teaching force in the country enjoys. It is worth studying a country that values education as Singapore does and yet does not include early childhood education in their narrative, policies, structure, and practices.

How does Singapore address the needs of students with special needs, special learning needs, or those with special rights?

The second theme that was not included in any of our presentations and which was not addressed in a coherent way when asked about was the theme of working with the population of students in the country with special needs. The very first, quick, answer I would get when I asked was that, "Teachers know how to work with the gifted in their classroom." When pressed to talk about children with dyslexia, autism, Down syndrome, or some other form of special learning needs, who some educators in the United States are referring to as "children with special rights," the answer I got was that those students were in special schools. Who prepares the teachers who work in those schools was, once again, a question I did not receive a clear answer for. There was no consistency, no clear message, and no unified answer about teacher preparation in this area. Instead, I heard, "There are some courses teachers can take" or "They get some professional development courses," or some other vague answer, vague by comparison with the straightforward clear answers about the "regular" K-12 system. This is another area I believe needs to be explored in more detail so than we can have a more complete understanding of the entire education system of Singapore and the preparation that the entire teaching workforce receives.

According to a teacher who spoke with us, international schools have better prepared special educators than any regular public school in Singapore. We did not hear where those teachers are prepared, but I assume they come from the countries of origin of those international schools. The separation of students with special needs—even moderate ones—from the regular public schools classmates is intriguing on a number of levels, but one quick question that I believe merits addressing is this: When international tests are given in the country, the population that takes the tests is the population of regular public school student. In the United States, those regular public school students include students with identified special needs. Apparently, that is not as common in Singapore. How can we use statistics to compare both countries when the populations that are assessed are different because of the design of each system?

Singapore is definitely a country that is committed to its population, to its development and well-being, to its education system, and thus to its teachers. It is worth studying, and I am grateful to the many professionals in Singapore who welcomed us, explained their policies and practices clearly, and who gave us the opportunity to learn from the best.

LETTER 6. REFLECTIONS ON SINGAPORE: AN ECOLOGY OF COHERENCE

— BY DAVID LUSSIER, EDD
Superintendent, Wellesley Public Schools

The perspective of an American superintendent –
Preconceived notions of a top-down system –
Teacher recruitment and support –
Nation building – The absence of a focus on teacher evaluation –
Leadership development – A coherent model
of human capital development

As the superintendent of a school district charged with preparing students to be successful in a 21st century global economy, I was extremely interested in learning more about the education system in Singapore, which has consistently received high marks on international benchmarks such as the Program for International Assessment (PISA). In October 2015, I joined a group of educators and colleagues working in education policy for a weeklong visit to this Asian city-state.

I must admit that one of my preconceived notions about Singapore was that it would be a highly centralized, top-down system that focused on a narrowly defined set of knowledge and skills. Instead, I found myself surprised to learn that the Singapore system is one based on a keen understanding of and significant investment in human capital development, which appears to be the engine of this remarkable education system.

Starting with the recruitment of top candidates for teaching positions, Singapore is impressive in how it links pre-service and in-service experiences. I was particularly struck by the thoughtfulness of the National Institute of Education (NIE), which oversees teacher and leadership preparation. In the United States, these functions tend to be discrete activities that are often compartmentalized in practice. The result is that teacher and leadership preparation are often thought about separately and can be disconnected from the experiences and needs of practitioners in the field.

In Singapore, educator preparation at the university level is linked more seamlessly with school-based practice. It appears that teachers command a great deal of respect in society and, as a result, the profession attracts a very high caliber of candidates. Aside from their coursework through the NIE, the work of student teachers is very much on the radar of the principals with whom we engaged. I sensed a far greater sense of responsibility at the school level for ensuring a high level of support for teachers in training than what we often see in the United States. This has the added benefit of creating a continuity of support once teachers make the transition to in-service experiences. Each of these beginning teachers receives a mentor and is closely supported by the staff and administrators in the building. While new teacher support is growing in the United States, it is not nearly as robust as what is currently in place in Singapore.

There is also a great deal of attention paid in Singapore to connecting the work of their staff to nation building. Quite literally, "The Ethos of the Teaching Profession," as they call it, includes the idea that, "We lead, care, inspire, for the future of the nation passes through our hands." (Wooi, Chan Yew. 2015. Presentation) This combination of high-quality training coupled with an exuberant sense of nationalism is a powerful combination for developing educators who feel a connection between their work in classrooms and the fate of the nation.

A facet of the teaching profession that I noticed was absent in Singapore was a focus and/or pressure to evaluate teachers. Their theory of action appears to be that if they attract high quality candidates and invest in their ongoing development, they will create and maintain a high caliber of teachers throughout the entire system. This stands in stark contrast to the United States, where entry into the teaching profession is relatively easy and support is highly variable. The result is a tremendous amount of pressure nationally to develop sophisticated evaluation systems to identify and dismiss poor performing teachers. This remains an extremely divisive wedge issue in American education.

Leadership development in Singapore is as impressive as teacher preparation, and is guided by a similar philosophy. The best teachers are typically identified early in their careers and then groomed for numerous leadership opportunities at the school level, NIE, and even the Ministry of Education. During our visit to the Academy of Singapore Teachers, we learned of a multi-track approach in which teachers may stay on a teacher track that includes positions such as senior teacher, lead teacher, master teacher, and principal master teacher. The leadership track includes positions such as department head, principal, and cluster superintendent. Rather than a career ladder, the Singapore model resembles more of a career lattice with movement in multiple directions. With so many opportunities for advancement that validates one's expertise, it's no wonder that teacher attrition is low!

Another example of Singapore's strategic investment in human capital is the NIE Leaders in Education Programme and its Creative Action Project (CAP). The leadership candidates participating in this program have to imagine what their "attachment" school will look like in 10-15 years, and then work with the current staff to implement one facet of this future school. What a great activity that challenges their sense of education trajectory, interpersonal skills, and project management expertise!

The degree to which Singapore reflects a coherent model of human capital development was perhaps my most significant take-away during our visit. Of course, as a city-state, they have far fewer political obstacles to shift from theory into practice than we do we in our decentralized system in the United States. Still, to see system that serves more than 300,000 students move with such clarity of purpose was inspiring to a superintendent who serves only 5,000 students!

Coincidentally, a few weeks after returning from Singapore, I attended a leadership conference in Washington, D.C. that included a panel conversation on education. One of the panelists is the current superintendent of a large urban district. Toward the end of the discussion, the moderator asked the panelists if they were paying attention to the approach of some of the most high-performing countries such as Singapore. The superintendent's response was that she was more concerned with the daily challenge of ensuring that her kids actually come to school to get them off of the streets. In many ways, I understand this response, which reflects the reality of the work in urban education. At the same time, after my visit to Singapore, I think there is so much that we can learn from their wise approach to teacher and leadership quality that is driven less by test-based accountability and more by strategic investments in training and development. These approaches are obviously resulting in significant dividends!

LETTER 7. OBSERVATIONS FROM THE DEAN OF A COLLEGE OF EDUCATION

— By CHRISTINE B. McCORMICK, PhD
Dean of the College of Education,
University of Massachusetts Amherst

Gratitude – Cultural values – Commitment –
Multiculturalism – Continuous improvement –
High stakes testing – Technical education

I would like to start by thanking those who organized this trip and made it possible for me to visit Singapore to study its educational system, overall, and the preparation of its educators, in particular. I would also like to extend my gratitude to those in Singapore who were generous with their time and expertise as they met with the "Delegation from Massachusetts," and who patiently answered a multitude of questions.

As the Dean of the College of Education at the University of Massachusetts Amherst, I was processing my experiences through the lens of an administrator at a flagship public research institution that prepares educators as one part of its mission. I also drew upon my decades of experience in teaching concepts of educational psychology and principles of child and adolescent development to pre-service teachers at other flagship universities in other regions of the United States (including the University of South Carolina and the University of New Mexico) in order to interpret what I was seeing and hearing. Finally, no doubt my experiences as the mother of a child with special educational needs influenced my perceptions.

The most striking take-home message from our trip was how strongly and deeply cultural values shape the Singaporean educational system. The high value placed on education, generally, and for the career path of teaching, specifically, was evident in the conversations we had everywhere we went. We can see the impact not only in the funding made available to education – as reflected in the physical layout of the schools themselves, in the quality of technological resources available in the schools, in the financial support for those pursuing careers in education, and, not insignificantly, in the salaries earned by educators – but also in the prestige accorded to those who pursue careers in education. Teachers are regarded as "nation builders," and as central to the success of the country at large. This commitment to education, and to being part of a worthwhile endeavor bigger than oneself, is underscored in the commitment ceremony for pre-service teachers, and in the symbolism of the compass given to each new teacher at the conclusion of the ceremony (and also given generously to us near the end of our trip).

Another significant way in which shared values manifest themselves in the Singaporean educational system is the manner in which choices made in educational policy and practice reflect how multiculturalism is embraced by society. For example, we were told – and could see – that personnel in the schools reflect the cultural mix of the communities they serve. In addition, the educational system actively supports the continuation of a multilingual society by requiring that students achieve proficiency not only in the state language, English, but also in their mother tongue.

Our discussions with officials in the Ministry of Education and in the National Institute of Education highlighted the commitment to continuous improvement that underlies the educational system. Research informs practice, and the close working relationship between the Ministry and the Institute enables changes to be introduced relatively quickly. Moreover, conversations with school leaders indicated that teachers are empowered to innovate and to share successful innovations with their colleagues. Educators in Singapore have opportunities to participate in programs to develop leadership and other areas of expertise as part of a clearly articulated pathway for professional development provided by the National Institute of Education. Thus, the continual emphasis on innovation and improvement extends beyond pedagogy to personnel.

As the dean of an institution of higher education whose programs have been nationally accredited since 1962, hearing about the speed with which changes can be enacted in Singapore made me envious. Although national accreditation in the United States does emphasize continuous improvement, in reality the context in which we work makes experimentation and innovation difficult. The articulated standards and criteria outlined in the national accreditation and state approval process are key to ensuring high quality preparation, and the intention is to encourage continuous improvement. Unfortunately, however, in practice and in policy, the accreditation and approval process makes teacher education programs less flexible and limits the ability to enact changes and evaluate outcomes in the spirit of continuous improvement.

Perhaps the most salient aspect of education in Singapore to us in the United States is the reliance on a truly high stakes testing program. High stakes in the sense that students' performance on the test taken at the end of sixth grade, the Primary School Leaving Exam (PSLE), is used to stream them into specific educational paths. We were given flow charts that indicated that there are opportunities for students to change course once they are streamed, but I had the impression that such movement was not commonplace. Some of the people we spoke to outside of the Ministry of Education and the National Institute of Education described the high stakes testing program as "destructive" and "soul-killing." We heard about parents seeking to enroll their students in the few independent schools where the tests are not required, and some parents shared with us their desire to emigrate so their children would not have to face the stress and sense of failure that they, themselves, experienced. Perhaps, ironically, educators from other countries visit Singapore because of the consistent high performance of Singaporean students on international tests of academic achievement (e.g., the PISA), yet the high stakes nature of the testing program in Singapore can be jarring, especially for those visitors from countries who do not employ their own high stakes testing programs.

My doctoral minor was in statistics and measurement, and the UMass Amherst College of Education has an exceptionally strong program in psychometrics and a highly successful Center for Educational Assessment. Our faculty have conducted validity studies for state (Massachusetts Comprehensive Assessment System [MCAS]) and national (National Assessment of Educational Progress [NAEP]) tests, served as consultants to developers of the Smarter Balance and PARCC assessments, and helped Indonesia develop its testing system. I do believe well-conceived and thoughtfully implemented testing programs can enhance educational opportunity and outcomes. However, I left Singapore with some unanswered questions about its testing program: We were informed that the test results are used to assess student proficiencies and not used to evaluate teacher effectiveness. Are the tests results, however, used to inform teaching practice and to evaluate pedagogy in the spirit of continuous improvement? Are students and parents provided formative feedback at any point in the process?

We learned through our conversations and by reading recent articles about the educational system that there is a current shift in Singapore to focus on the whole child and to foster the development of 21st century thinking skills. We did not, however, have the opportunity to observe classroom instruction to see firsthand implementation of this new approach. I would have been particularly interested in this given my long time interest in strategy instruction and the development of metacognition – a component of 21st century skills. Our group would have also been very interested to see how a teacher manages classes of around 40 students, since this is considered large by U.S. standards. We did, however, have the opportunity to observe another reform we had read about: a renewed investment in the technical and vocational education track. We visited a technical high school and observed students who appeared to be highly engaged in their study and associated hands-on activities, such as filming a movie or repairing a passenger jet. The sprawling, attractive facility was impressive, providing a variety of opportunities for students to develop readiness for the workforce, particularly for careers requiring 21st century technology skills.

Throughout our visit, we were reminded about the level of interaction between school leaders, the Ministry of Education and the Institute of Education. Yet, I could not help but note that the tone sometimes used when someone mentioned "The Ministry" was very much like what I hear on our campus when someone mentioned "The Administration." Not surprisingly, this was especially true in our conversation with union leaders. So no matter how far you go – even to the other side of the world – some things remain the same.

In preparation for this trip, we read portions of *From Third World to First*, a book written by founding prime minister Lee Kuan Yew. On many occasions, our hosts reverently invoked Mr. Yew's name. The intensity of the reverence would have seemed overblown if I hadn't been exposed to the ideas outlined in his book. The transformation of Singapore over the last 50 years is remarkable, and a great deal of the economic development has resulted from the investment in education, a cornerstone of Mr. Yew's vision. The investment in education fuels the spirit of continuous improvement that transformed Singapore.

LETTER 8. A SYSTEMIC AND SYSTEMATIC APPROACH TO TEACHING AND LEARNING: PLAYING THE LONG GAME IN EDUCATION

— By CONNIE K. CHUNG, EdD
Research Director, Global Education
Innovation Initiative, Harvard Graduate
School of Education

How systems support 21ˢᵗ century teaching and learning in Singapore –
Singapore's ambitious and comprehensive learning goals for students –
Playing the long game in the United States –

In October 2015, I visited Singapore with colleagues from Massachusetts who are leaders of universities, foundations, research organizations, and nonprofits working in education. We focused on learning about Singapore's education system during our five-day visit. I highlight below a few thoughts from our trip.

The key difference between our education system in the United States and the Singaporean system is that while we think and invest in individuals and programs, aware of our short political, policy, and funding cycles, Singaporeans think and invest in systems, taking advantage of their longer term political and policy cycles. I draw this thesis from a few observations made on the trip, outlined below.

1. How systems support 21ˢᵗ century teaching and learning in Singapore

Singaporean teachers enter a highly developed, thoughtfully constructed system of training and selection that tracks, supports, and develops them. While there is a high bar for entry into the profession, and a rigorous evaluation of teachers that includes a way to dismiss low performing teachers, once a teacher enters a teacher preparation program, there is a clearly articulated pathway for professional growth, as a master teacher, school leader, or subject specialist. Teacher retention levels are high, and only 3% of the teachers leave each year[14]. Regular and systematic transfer of personnel among the Ministry of Education, schools, teacher preparation and research institutions also ensure that practice, policy, and preparation are tightly linked in the city-state; that there is a high likelihood that what teachers learn in their preparation programs is aligned with what they will actually need to do in the classroom; and that policymakers and researchers have practitioners' points of view in mind as they develop policy and design their research agendas.

Furthermore, in Singapore, there is an assumption that teaching well is a highly demanding and skilled work, requiring systematic cultivation and support. Thus, policymakers appear to focus their attention on developing a system that will identify and support better learning and teaching in their schools, rather than on methods to reward and punish individual teachers, schools, and districts as the primary lever of change. For example, they recently established the Academy of Singapore Teachers that builds a "teacher-led culture of professional excellence centered on the holistic development of the child" in their schools.[15] Individual teachers may have weaknesses, but the overwhelming strength of the Singaporean system of professional development appears to be designed to compensate for those shortcomings, ensuring that students will have a good chance of encountering effective teachers.

Similarly, Singapore's educational *practices* are part of a system, knitted together under a single comprehensive national framework and a series of long-term national strategies for teaching and learning. During our trip, we were told about the history of Singapore, with the identification of four key periods of educational policy that led to the development of the current education system, with each period lasting 14 to 17 years. This relatively long-term, system-wide and systematic approach education ensures that principals and teachers in Singapore have the

---

[14] Personal communication, Dr. Ee-Ling Low, Head of Office of Strategic Planning and Academic Quality, National Institution of Education, 2015.

[15] http://www.moe.gov.sg/about/org-structure/academy/

opportunity to not just know the driving principles and key ideas for the system, but also have the time and resources with which to put them to practice and execute them.

For example, on our trip we visited the Crescent Girls School, where the principal was piloting new ways to use technology in the classroom. She was not just helping her teachers and students experience new ways of learning, not just following the latest entrepreneurial idea she had picked up from her days at Stanford, and not just ensuring that her schools remained attractive to parents and funders. Instead, because her school was a designated pilot school tasked with finding ways other schools in Singapore might more effectively use technology in their classrooms, she had a wealth of new equipment and support staff to assist her in implementing her ideas, including the funding to form a partnership with a research organization at Stanford to assess their progress in this work. The decisions made by the principal as a building leader appear to have been informed by a larger, unifying vision and coherent education strategy for the country as a whole, which allowed room for innovation and improvement. Under such a coherent system of practice, goals and principles are not just talking and advocacy points but are supported with human and financial resources; thus, they have a higher chance of not just being implemented, but of being developed into good practices, refined over a period of years, and then spread to other schools throughout the education system[16].

---

[16] Because our time in Singapore was so short, I'm not sure to what degree these resources are equitably distributed among the different schools and neighborhoods; but overall, in general, there appears to be an explicit effort to support students, including the creation of special schools for students at risk of dropping out, such as the NorthLight School, and the Institute of Technical Education to support those who are sorted into vocational schools. Also, the brevity of this letter precludes me from expressing the concerns and drawbacks I see in the Singaporean education system and the benefits I see in the US system, so I submit this letter knowing that it may read as being too laudatory of one, and too detractive of the other.

2. Singapore's ambitious and comprehensive learning goals for students

Perhaps because they have the luxury of knowing that they have an entire system behind them, Singapore's education leaders take on ambitious and comprehensive learning goals for their students. They explicitly plan for and aim to provide an education to their students that is expansive and responsive to the changing local and global contexts, including past, present, and future needs, challenges, and opportunities in their country and in the world. We saw these aspirations as our visit coincided with Singapore's celebration of its 50th anniversary "as one people"[17] and less than a year after the passing of its founding Prime Minister, Lee Kwan Yew. During our visit, we saw colorful banners adorning the streets to celebrate this anniversary and heard presenters who spoke of the race riots between the Malays and the Chinese that Singapore had experienced 50 years earlier, and how they deliberately focus their efforts to ensure that the current mix of Chinese, Malay, Indians, Christians, Muslims, Hindus and other ethnic and religious groups would live well together. We found out that Singapore's "desired student outcomes" for all of their students include being "a concerned citizen," an "active contributor," with "civic literacy, global awareness and cross-cultural skills."[18]

For example, during our trip, we attended a student fair, where students training for educational management positions presented what they had learned about other countries' education systems after self-organizing trips to these countries. We also learned that their principal training program includes the exercise of envisioning what Singapore might look like in 20 years and thinking about how to align their schools to meet the challenges and opportunities of the future. Thus, I had the distinct impression, at least from our trip, that Singaporean education leaders at all levels were keenly aware of their history, continually thought

[17] https://www.singapore50.sg
[18] http://www.moe.gov.sg/education/desired-outcomes/

about the future, and used the present to nurture their students and organizations so that the country would be well prepared to thrive.

3. Playing the long game in the United States

Not having had the opportunity to visit a Singaporean classroom during the trip, however, I do not know to what degree these principles and values are actually taught to Singaporean students. But, I do know that in the United States, we have educators who are keenly aware of the racial tensions in our country's history, who are mindful of the pressing need to teach students about other parts of the planet even as our world becomes more globalized, and the need to make education relevant, rigorous, and responsive to present and future challenges such as concerns about the environment, peace and security, and widening inequality; they also work effectively to address these concerns in the classroom. In fact, I'd posit that organizations such as Facing History and Ourselves, the Asia Society, and Expeditionary Learning/EL Education, among many others, do well in developing curricula and resources to support many of the same goals that the Singaporean system espouses.

What we do not see as much in the United States, however, is a sustained and large-scale effort to implement such programs at the systems level, and the effort to command the necessary financial and human resources to do so. We let our schools scramble for ad hoc funding and support from foundations and nonprofits, on short policy and programmatic cycles. For example, the average tenure of a US superintendent fluctuated from 2.8 years in 2008 to 3.18 years in 2014, according to the Council of Great City Schools[19], and funding cycles do not run in decades but in months and years. Under such short leadership, policy, and funding cycles – and with shifting priorities and the overwhelming pressure to align organizational goals and resources solely to produce measurable

---

[19] http://blogs.edweek.org/edweek/District_Dossier/2014/11/urban_school _superintendent_te.html

results – schools and programs tend to focus on efforts that produce short-term gains aligned to narrow goals.

As a result, we have a plethora of organizations that focus not only on a small area of concern, but on one facet of one aspect of one small area of concern, making advocacy our priority, rather than coordination, coherence, alignment, effective implementation, and systemic/ systematic improvement. After 20 years spent in education, both as a classroom teacher and a researcher speaking with practitioners, I have made the claim to colleagues in the past that in such a context, an unofficial but nevertheless a critical competency of a "good" principal and superintendent in the US is the ability to create the political room for their staff to invest in long-term, sustained improvement efforts, to "protect" them from the buffeting winds of policy priorities that appear to change every 2-3 years, and to stay in their jobs long enough to build relationships with community members and organizations that are critical to marshaling the resources necessary to sustain an excellent school and district.

My thoughts in this letter are reflective not just of our trip, but also come from having worked with colleagues from the National Institute of Education in Singapore and from research institutions in four other countries over the last two years, as part of my work at the Harvard Graduate School of Education's Global Education Innovation Initiative. We just finished writing a book about the goals and purposes of education in the 21st century in six nations, and are writing our second book together about exemplary programs[20] in seven countries that are making an effort to teach students the competencies they will need to thrive in the 21st century. One of the preliminary findings from our second book might be that the kind of project-based teaching and learning that is relevant to developing in students not just STEM/STEAM competencies but the interpersonal and intrapersonal competencies

---

[20] We first looked for systems, but could not find them, so looked to programs.

necessary to thrive in our present world, requires the efforts of not just individual teachers and schools, but of teams of teachers, networks of schools, multiple stakeholders including teacher education and principal training programs, private foundations, and entire educational systems. Perhaps with these letters from Singapore, we can instigate the kind of conversations and activities that will lead to continuing to develop in Massachusetts and in the United States a systemic and systematic approach to teaching and learning, so that policymakers and education leaders are encouraged to play the long game.

LETTER 9. PURPOSES, PROFESSIONALS, AND POLICIES IN ACTION

— By MITALENE FLETCHER, PhD

Director of K-12 and International Programs,
Programs for Professional Education,
Harvard Graduate School of Education

Purpose – Engineer, doctor, or teacher – Language matters? –
No Child Left Behind - Singapore style – Impressions and questions

Our weeklong study tour of Singapore's renowned education system left me with four strong impressions and a deeper appreciation of my most basic questions concerning the purpose of education, the role and status of teachers, and how we, as a community of educators, build and sustain a more equitable society.

1. Purpose

We were welcomed by faculty from the National Institute of Education (NIE), which is nestled in a quiet, bucolic corner of Nanyang Technological University in the southwestern part of Singapore. Our visit there coincided with a celebration of students' recent time abroad. These students were on leave from their posts as department heads and enrolled in the four-month Management & Leadership in Schools (MLS) program, which included a two-week study tour, all fully funded by the Ministry of Education. The celebration was a festival of sorts, in which students posted images and reflections from their time abroad, and offered us samples of the local delicacies they brought back. NIE's associate dean for leadership Programs, Pak Tee Ng, made remarks of congratulation and provided a powerful example of the way teachers are inducted and held in a fraternity with a mission to build the nation. He reminisced about his own travels to Thailand where he visited a head teacher and staff with few resources to speak of, but with the determination to teach the skills students would need to lift themselves out of poverty and beyond. Pak Tee turned this into a story of nation-building and reminded those gathered of their roles in this project – in their schools, in the education system, and in the broader society.

2. Engineer, Doctor, or Teacher

Each day, we learned more about how Singapore nurtures the professionalism of teachers through its policies, practices, and system of beliefs. There are multiple tracks for teachers to advance in their careers and gain status and recognition: they may become content specialists, attain the status of master teachers, or they may be recruited into the leadership track. For the first two, the Ministry supports 100 hours of professional development each year and operates a thriving academy for ongoing development. The NIE also offers an array of programs, some offering credentials, such as the MLS.

Initial teacher preparation is competitive, with the NIE admitting only 20% of applicants – all of whom are already college graduates – into the Post Graduate Certificate in Education. Once admitted, trainees are paid whilst studying and upon entering the workforce, and earn as much as newly-minted doctors, engineers and other professionals. The latest Ministry initiative for teacher recruitment is the Teacher Scholar Program, enticing the brightest secondary school graduates straight into initial teacher preparation.

In our pre-travel reading, as well as during our short stay, we were struck by the message of high expectations for teachers in promoting national values and in building Singapore's human resources, and we were impressed with the systems of support and reward. "Each year, teachers are very happy in July and December, " declared the general secretary of Singapore Teachers' Union in a frank and engaging discussion. It is at those points in the year when teachers and other civil servants are paid the "annual variable component" of their salary – a bonus based on Singapore's economic performance. Teachers are also eligible for individual performance bonuses of up to two months' pay.

(And even though freedom of the press is a value that Americans hold dear, I have to admit my delight in learning that the press is not permitted to criticize or undermine the work of teachers.)

Furthermore, the education system is dynamic and "porous." Principals are transferred every seven years, and both teachers and principals are seconded to the Ministry of Education to support policy development and then sent back into schools. There also seems to be endless funding for teachers to take leave and earn graduate degrees abroad.

As a consequence of this (and, of course, more variables in the social and political ecology), the attrition rate for teachers in Singapore is less than 4%, and less than 1% for students, and we are all aware that Singapore has made headlines for its students' academic performance.

Could some of Singapore's methods inspire practices that improve conditions for teachers and lead to better outcomes for students in Massachusetts? For example, the idea of a dynamic and porous system is compelling as a way to make sure that expertise flows up and across a system. Rather than initiatives that assign teachers with minimal training and experience to high-need schools, I would love to see initiatives that recruit teachers with deep experience and a track record of success, provide them with specialized training (perhaps in differentiated instruction, strategies for creating a culture of thinking, etc.), and send *them* to high-need schools in Massachusetts. A monetary incentive might be required, but perhaps a patriotic incentive - knowing that Massachusetts will not realize its greatest potential with 2%, or roughly 6,000 students, dropping out annually[21] would be enough.

3. Language Matters?

By mid-week, our American baggage had grown heavy. Over the seventeen years I have lived in the United States, a colorful word cloud representing the discourse of American education has solidified in my mind: "Underperforming + Failing + Schools + Black + Latino +

[21] Massachusetts Department of Elementary and Secondary Education, School Dropout Rates in Massachusetts Public Schools 2013-14, http://www.doe.mass.edu/infoservices/reports/dropout/2013-2014/

Poor + Urban + ..." These words are uttered together with disturbing frequency by educators, political leaders, social commentators, and the like, and the cloud is hard to shake off—even after flying 27 hours. I was not the only one growing slightly suspicious when host after gracious host told us that "In Singapore, every school is a good school" and "There must be racial harmony and it cannot be taken for granted." We could not resist asking questions about test scores and social stratification. Sing Kong Lee, Vice President of Nanyang Technical University, readily admitted, "There is one group that does not perform as well as other groups in math..." He did not indicate which racial group, but went straight on to explain the constellation of strategies and support for improving social conditions and addressing test results. Later in the week, we asked again about low performing and failing schools. Our hosts at the Academy of Singapore Teachers seemed perplexed by our terminology and explained that they do not use the term "low performing." Instead, they look at the profile of students in any given school and see how educators are serving them. Based on findings, the Ministry then gives these schools more social workers and more support from family services.

By simply rejecting the term "low performing" do you realize your vision that "every school is a good school?" Doubtful. However, it was refreshing to spend a week under a brand new "word cloud," and I wish that Massachusetts could lead our nation in promoting new language to analyze what high-performing students do and have (and to allocate resources to spread these conditions), and to focus less on what low performing students, on average, look like – because, as we began to learn in Singapore, that's not the point.

4. No Child Left Behind – *Singapore Style*

On our final day, we set out for one last visit, traveling along the well-paved highways and through the pristine streets, busy with construction, and arrived at the Institute for Technical Education (ITE), a sprawling, modern building, barely a decade old. The hallways were twenty feet wide with soaring ceilings. The light-filled building was designed to integrate natural ecology, including a shallow stream that ran the length of an atrium and gigantic plant beds where 30-foot tall trees stood amongst thickets of crotons, small ficus trees and ferns.

The building was also designed to integrate the public and demonstrate the importance of vocational and technical education. Thus the lower level is a shopping mall with a café, flower shop, and gift shop all run by students selling goods they created. At the far end of the atrium was a marine technology training center with massive generators and engines typically found on cargo ships. Signs acknowledged generous sponsorship from engineering firms. Across the way we found facilities for the avionics program, equipped with real aircraft as well as a flight simulator and the model of an aircraft's interior, all so that students can practice all of the functions of preparing and repairing an aircraft for flight and serving passengers from their arrival at the airport to their landing.

This significant investment in ITE benefits the 25% of each school cohort in Singapore who were outperformed by their peers on the Primary School Leaving Exam and who were tracked into the vocational and technical track. These students complete four years of secondary school and then two years of career-oriented technical training with internship placements. Consequently, when students graduate they move straight into full-time jobs. Singapore's unemployment rate is 1%. The facilities, resources, and aesthetics of ITE communicate that all students deserve the opportunity and support needed to acquire the skills to make a good living and to contribute to society. Our experience at ITE reminded me of Pak Tee Ng's remarks earlier that week. He explained that while there is no explicit "no child left behind" policy from the Ministry, Singapore's current (low) birthrate of 1.7 and the size and skill profile of the workforce required to advance Singapore means that, "we cannot afford to practice otherwise."

Our group of travelers comprised researchers and leaders from Massachusetts' higher education, K-12 system, non-profits, and foundations – a group with diverse perspectives but a common mission. We reflected on our observations and analyses together, and I emerged with the following impressions and questions. Singapore is inspiring because of its clarity of purpose throughout the education system and for its cultural and political context that depends on and invests wholeheartedly in education. What would it mean for Massachusetts to have a thriving economy and society that serves all residents well? What industries, job skills, and cultural norms would Massachusetts need to have to achieve full employment? Finally, how can education enable all of this?

Letter 10. The Quest to Find Out What is "Normal" in Singapore

— By Lisa Battaglino, PhD
Dean of the College of Education and Allied Studies, Bridgewater State University

Relaxed – Technology – What is "normal?" – Cultivating talent – Students with disabilities – Comparison with the United States – Flawed, but no better system

As the Massachusetts delegation quietly made their way through the Crescent Girls School library in Singapore, there was little doubt the yellow-bloused pre-teens were relaxed, unfazed by visitors, and comfortably engaged in their studies. There was no teacher patrolling nor a stern librarian observing their studies, and there were few books visible. Instead, the girls each held a tablet device to scan their notes while conversing in hushed and happy tones. The twelve-year-olds looked like Wellesley College women prepping for midterms more than they resembled adolescents preparing for a high stakes test. This appeared to be the norm for those privileged to attend the elite public exam school.

In her presentation to us, the dynamo 5-foot-tall principal of the school called the girls her "darlings" and described the school as an idyllic environment that fostered a culture of excellence. While schools in the U.S. often lack infrastructures to support computers, the Crescent Girls School enjoys a plethora of current innovations. The technology was unlike any available in typical public schools in the United States. In one classroom, ten enormous five foot square prone models of the most advanced type of multi-touch interactive tablets appeared. The related game options were specifically designed by the teachers in conjunction with the ample tech staff to reflect the needs of the curriculum and to encourage groups of four children to simultaneously interact in realistic visual and auditory activities. In addition, they regularly used MoNet Lab (a mobile networking lab) for digital art and music and Chromakey technology, an interactive immersive virtual reality where teachers use a device including a camera to place a student into a virtual reality image. The student is able to watch herself in the virtual reality interacting with other students or three dimensional virtual figures. Video conferencing and iMedia were also in frequent use. All of these undertakings were fully supported by a ten person full-time highly skilled tech staff to ensure optimal function. To my eyes, it seemed almost too good to be true, so I began a quest to discover whether Crescent Girls School reflected the norm, or whether it is a unique example of what Singapore provides for their best and brightest students.

Detailed presentations by members of the hierarchy of the Singapore National Institute of Education, the Ministry of Education, and the Academy of Singapore Teachers revealed a clearly organized and research-based transparent process for preparing teachers, master teachers, and principals. Our tour guide at the National Institute of Education labeled it "cultivating talent and building a professional education system." It was impressive in its well thought-out details and research-based principles, and still surprisingly similar to the teacher preparation process in Massachusetts. Basically, the only major differences between their techniques to prepare teachers and Massachusetts' practices are a pervasive focus on future thinking and the philosophy that teachers are "nation builders." However, I was hesitant to accept that these relatively minor differences in teacher preparation methods could have resulted in creating a school system that is thought to be the finest in the world in identifying, developing, and supporting faculty, administrators and staff. I thought there must be another explanation for the system's achievements.

The experts we spoke to described extraordinary and desirable accomplishments of the educational system, but when asked about how the system serves children with disabilities, these leaders evaded direct responses besides mentioning there are two public schools (out of their 800 school structures) that these children may attend. It was clear to me that full inclusion and early intervention do not appear to be widely accepted concepts. In a young country such as this one, segregating students with disabilities would not be surprising if it were not for the fact that Singaporean educational leaders boast of ethnic harmony while apparently having no such consideration for diverse learners. Undeniably, Singaporeans are succeeding in preparing effective future teachers and school leaders, and I commend their commitment to esteeming teachers, paying teachers at the same level as engineers, generously funding schools, and providing infrastructure to support modern classrooms, especially since these attitudes and practices provide a critical foundation for schools that is often lacking in the U.S. However, screening students, tracking students (or streaming as Singaporeans say), implementing high stakes testing starting at 12 years old (in the form of the Primary School Leaving Test [PSLT]), fostering a national sense of dread and stress that requires private tutoring for all students, and marginalizing persons with disabilities in society are practices unacceptable in the U.S.

One night during the visit, an expatriate met us for dinner. He has lived in Singapore for many years and has raised his family there with his Singaporean wife, whom he met in the States while in college. He explained that the public school system in Singapore is tough and that his children would probably find it too difficult to navigate. Pressure to do well, the competition amongst children to score high on exams which govern their future, the high cost of out of school tutorials, and a relentless rigor that leaves little time for anything more than schoolwork forced him to choose private school options for his family. Albeit, he did say that though the school system, along with the government, is far from perfect, he knows of no better system in the world.

As a U.S. college of education administrator, I spend part of each day meeting with partners who work in inner city American schools. They are typically underfunded, deficient in material and human resources, have little or no instructional technology support, and grapple with the daily dilemmas of hungry children, unacceptable student behaviors, drug issues, fear of school shootings, and low teacher morale. The idea of a public school system, such as that of Singapore, having the luxury of teaching masses of children in state of the art classrooms with energized, motivated, highly educated and well paid teachers is appealing and enviable. There is no utopia for education, but as flawed as it may be, it would be foolish to ignore the strong success Singapore is enjoying in terms of their teacher preparation, effective school system, student achievement, strong economy, and reputation as an international educational trailblazer. Since it is the goal of U.S. education leaders to create schools where children learn and thrive and where teenagers graduate ready to excel in college or the workplace, we are in no position to ignore Singapore's example.

One could argue that Singapore does not focus on educating *all* children equally, as we commendably have attempted to do in the U.S. since the 1975 enactment of Public Law 94-142 (now IDEA). Moreover, compared to the U.S. their country is very small. But, Singapore is legitimately due bragging rights regarding their educational and economic advances. Fortunately, they seem eager to share their concepts, techniques, and experiences with the rest of the world, including through hosting delegations such as ours. Their immaculate streets and sidewalks, incredibly low crime rate, nearly drug-free society, strong Confucian philosophy, high gross national income, and elevated respect for teachers combine to produce an enviable environment for educators and teacher preparation programs. In the end, I left with a sense that the Crescent Girls School may be an unsurpassed model in an exceptional system and not necessarily the norm, but this does not diminish the fact that great things are being done in *all* of Singapore, and that they have every reason to be viewed as having premier schools and teacher preparation systems.

Letter 11. Lessons on Coherence, Commitment, and Equity Far From Home

— By E. B. O'Donnell
Doctoral student,
Harvard Graduate School of Education

Reminders of home – Coherence – Commitment –
Equity – A new mindset

It is strange to be reminded of home when one is, quite literally, as far from home as possible. I have lived in the Boston area for over six years and outside of Texas for the last fourteen years, yet I suppose those foundational memories of sight, sound, smell, and climate persist and rise to the forefront when one is in unfamiliar territory. While the trees and vegetation were different, and the traffic moved on the left side of the road instead of the right, the similarities between my hometown of Houston and Singapore would not leave me.

Both are sprawling megacities with high humidity and abundant greenery. Both are multicultural, metropolitan and—perhaps appallingly—business-friendly. This similarity might not be surprising when one considers that both are built upon swamplands and both have grown exponentially in roughly the same time frame (Houston has nearly doubled in size[22] and Singapore has tripled since its independence in 1965[23]). Yet, the differences in what Singapore has *done* with that growth, that business-friendly mentality, and that diverse human capital is striking when one compares it with what has been done or could be done in a prosperous place like Houston or elsewhere in the United States.

Houston essentially does not do any city planning, it has virtually no zoning laws, and is said to be run by land developers (not the city

[22] Census.gov. (2016). State & County QuickFacts – Houston, TX. Retrieved February 25, 2016, from http://quickfacts.census.gov/qfd/states/48/4835000.html
[23] World Bank (2016). Data – Singapore. Retrieved February 25, 2016, from http://data.worldbank.org/country/singapore

government, unless they happen to be one in the same).[24] On the other hand, seemingly every detail of Singaporean society is centrally planned by the benevolent (they hope), if mysterious, powers-that-be. Houston Independent School District ranks 3,709th in the nation[25], while Singapore's public education system tops international assessments like the Programme for International Student Assessment (PISA) (ranking 2nd, behind Shanghai), Progress in International Reading Literacy Study (PIRLS) (ranking 4th, behind Hong Kong, Russia, and Finland), and Trends in International Math and Science Study (TIMSS) (ranking 1st in math and 2nd in science, behind Korea). Only 78% of Houstonians graduate from high school[26], versus 99% in Singapore[27].

What might account for these vast differences, and what might we learn from their example?

Coherence

First, due to the centralized nature and small size of the Singaporean system, there is amazing coherence between policies and programs. At times it was somewhat disconcerting to hear the same messages, the same phrases, and the same figures cited over and over during our week of visits and presentations. Since teachers and principals, it seemed, have the opportunity (if they so choose) to cycle into the ministry or National Institute of Education (NIE) for a few years before returning to the classroom/school, it appeared that the frontline

[24] In fact, the founders of Houston, the Allen brothers, set that precedent; they themselves were in the business of developing land for commercial purposes.
[25] Niche.com. (2016). 2016 Best School Districts - Niche. Retrieved January 31, 2016, from https://k12.niche.com/rankings/public-school-districts/best-overall/
[26] Houston Independent School District. (2015). Facts and Figures. Retrieved January 31, 2016 from http://www.houstonisd.org/Page/41879
[27] Singapore Ministry of Education. (2014). Student drop-out rate for Primary, Secondary and ITE levels. Retrieved January 31, 2016 from http://www.moe.gov.sg/media/parliamentary-replies/2014/04/student-drop-out-rate-for-primary-secondary-and-ite-levels.php

educators not only *heard* the messages sent to them from the central office, but often played a role in *creating* those messages and therefore *bought into* them. I have heard from colleagues and friends who teach or who study policy reform and implementation in the United States that there is frequently only a loose relationship between policies set at the district level and what is enacted in the classroom, and that this is often due to lack of teacher buy-in to the policy. What are the barriers to enacting a similar rotational program at the district level in Massachusetts, where teachers, administrators, and policymakers rotate in and out of levels of the system (the classroom, the school, and the district offices)? What could be the effects of the perspective one would gain from this kind of experience on the coherence of policies and implementation efforts?

Commitment

Second, in Singapore, there is a clear message about the value of education that is disseminated throughout all levels of the education system. Everyone from the top ministry officials to the vast majority of parents (it seemed[28]) touts the vital importance of educational success, even if they aren't always as thrilled about the lengths they and their children must go to succeed in school. We heard about parents who quit their full-time jobs to be an Uber driver the year before their child was to take the high stakes Primary School Leaving Exam (PSLE). As an Uber driver (or in a similar job), parents would have the flexibility to spend after-school hours helping their child study and prepare (through outside tuition, often) for the exam. We also heard that positive message about teachers were posted on all public buses in the place where, in the United States, ads for soda or toothpaste appear.

---

[28] Our delegation had very little opportunity to speak with parents about their beliefs about education. However, teachers, principals, and administrators all discussed the challenges and advantages of working with parents who put such pressure on their children to succeed academically.

This kind of commitment to and reverence for education from parents, teachers, administrators, central office planners, and the public stands in stark contrast to the way that we talk about teachers, parents, and schooling, in general, in the United States. For better or worse, the rise of alternative credentialing programs (like those associated with Teach for America) and charter school networks (like KIPP, which was founded in Houston and New York) signal both lack of faith in teaching as a profession, and a lack of faith in (traditional) public schools as an equitable and effective public institution. Because Singapore tightly regulates who can opt out of the public system[29], virtually all families and other stakeholders are invested in maintaining a high quality public education system.

While we likely wouldn't want American parents to go to the length of quitting their jobs to help their children study for a high-stakes exam, and it would be antithetical to American notions of freedom to limit access to private schooling for those who wish to attend them (and can afford the tuition), we may wish to ask ourselves how can we make sure that the public's emotional and resource investments into schools are encouraged and rewarded? How we might be able to create structures to get parents more active in their children's achievement? Some might argue that American parents just aren't as invested in education—that they just don't care—but evidence from the rising number of parents who are opting to roll the dice with charter school lotteries, for example, tells a different story. Moreover, barring pathology like addiction and cases of child abuse and neglect, I believe that parents universally want their children to succeed in school. We should think beyond Parent Teacher Associations, which are only loosely connected to achievement and which are not directly focused on the outcomes of their specific child. Some might also argue that some parents, who might not have been themselves successful in their schooling, might not be equipped

---

[29] My understanding is that parents must apply to the government for a waiver to send their child to parochial, international, or other independent school.

to actively participate in their child's academic achievement. Yet, ask adult Singaporeans whose parents had limited access to school about the academic encouragement (some of it punitive, however) that they received growing up. Perhaps if we respected and trusted parents and students more with their achievement, parents and students would be able to be the true partners in education that they wish to be.

Equity

Singapore is not immune from their own version of the achievement gap, yet the expectations are high for all learners and the strictly meritocratic system provides opportunities for advancement despite socio-economic disadvantage. Many of us in the delegation were somewhat uncomfortable with the early age at which children are sorted into separate tracks (high academic/pre-collegiate, academic/ polytechnic, and technical/vocational). In sixth grade, at around age 11, students take the PSLE, which determines the secondary school type and thus the child's future. We were, perhaps justly, critical of a system that failed to account for late bloomers or for an early period of low risk experimentation and exposure to curricular options for which the child might not have a natural aptitude.

However, in our country while we do not have this kind of early determinative exam and tracking, the reality is that the socio-economic circumstances and the zip code into which a child in America is born might be having a similar and possibly even more insidious effect. A child born into a poorer district is already likely sentenced to a non-college education track through the poor quality schools he or she is assigned to.

A new mindset

The five days I spent as a member of the Massachusetts delegation certainly generated a number of questions and ideas in my mind about what can be done closer to home to improve educational opportunities and outcomes for students. It seems clear to me, that while not all policies and programs of Singapore's system would be appropriate for our American context, there are many things that could be done with few resources, without drastic changes to educational policy, but instead with simply a new mindset about our commitment to equity, coherence, and excellence in our schools.

Letter 12. Clarity, Commitment, and Coherence

— By Vanessa Lipschitz

Portfolio Manager,
Jacobson Family Foundation

*Our group of Massachusetts education leaders – What
shaped my questions about the system –
Five elements that drive success – Mission and
role clarity – Sustained focus –
Consistency of communication – A top-quality
human capital management system –
Incentivized student and parent engagement –
Final reflections for an American context*

In October 2015, a group of colleagues working in different areas of the Massachusetts education system set off on a trip to Singapore to find out what we could learn from a small island nation on the other side of the world. The group comprised diverse perspectives: school and district officials, academics, nonprofit leaders, policymakers, teacher educators, and funders. Each was inclined to apply his or her own professional lens to the task of explaining the Singapore education system's differences from that of the US—a petri dish for Maslow's hammer explanations. My own perspective was shaped by my professional background as someone who has spent the past 10 years looking at both nonprofit and for-profit organizations to identify how they can best produce targeted results. It is a perspective that is oriented toward leading with diagnostic questions rather than strongly held beliefs.

In the case of Singapore, two sets of facts shaped these questions. The first, the fact that students in Singapore perform, on average, at the top of all countries that participated in the cross national assessment of student knowledge and skills conducted by the Organization of Economic Cooperation and Development in mathematics, reading and science[30]. The second, the documented positive correlation between the percentage of students who score at the higest levels in PISA and the perception teachers have of the extent to which teaching is a valued profession[31].

The historical context of Singapore makes the empirical results even more astounding. In the late 1950s, when Singapore was only a semi-independent British colony, around 70% of its economy was driven by port activities and the country had no knowledge economy. The baseline educational performance was lackluster; the literacy rate hovered around 50% for the population 15 and over with a legacy of education for only the most affluent.[32] The diverse mix of Chinese, Malay, English, and Tamil speakers seemed the perfect backdrop for progress-inhibiting ethnic division. Had Singapore gone on to achieve performance at OECD average levels, it would have been impressive; the fact that over the course of 50 years the country has become a chart-topping nation is awe-inspiring.

If the essential question is how, the simplest answers seem to be the clarity of purpose and the steadfast commitment that have driven exceptional coherence throughout the education system. Having spent time looking at some of our country's largest for-profit businesses, both as a student and as a strategy consultant, I have a profound appreciation for the complexity of setting and executing thoughtful strategy. Listening to Singaporeans,

---

[30] Organization of Economic Cooperation and Development (2012) *PISA Results in Focus: What 15-year-olds Know and What They Can Do with What They Know.* Available at http://www.oecd.org/pisa/keyfindings/pisa-2012-results.htm.

[31] Organization for Economic Cooperation and Development. *What helps teachers feel valued and satisfied with their jobs,* (OECD Teaching in Focus Series: Brief No. 5). Retrieved from http://www.oecd.org/edu/school/teachinginfocus.htm

[32] Dixon, C. (1991). *Southeast Asia and the World Economy.* Cambridge: Cambridge University Press. As cited in Boon, G.C. and Gopinathan, S. (2006). *The Development of the Singapore Education System since 1965.* Singapore: National Institute of Education; Wedgeworth, R. (1993). Singapore. In *World Encyclopedia of Library and Information Services.* (Third Edition, pp. 777). Chicago, Illinois: American Library Association.

ranging from government officials to school leaders, the country's ability to define a strategy and deliver corresponding results rivals some of the best companies in the United States. But "clarity," "commitment," and "coherence" are broad and amorphous concepts, and education is a policy arena where details matter. Based on the information and views gathered on the visit to Singapore, I would highlight five elements that seem to drive the success of the Singaporean system.

1. Mission and Role Clarity

From Singapore's founding as an independent nation, the mission of the education system has been clear: to produce a workforce capable of driving sustained economic growth to raise living standards. Countless individuals repeated the national narrative that begins with Singapore's position as a new nation with no natural resources and only its human capital on which to rely. As Singapore's founding father reiterated in *The Singapore Story: Memoirs of Lee Kuan Yew*: "After trying out a number of ways to reduce inequalities and failing, I was gradually forced to conclude that the decisive factors were the people, their natural abilities, education and training." It is this shared, core belief in the tie between education and economic success that has driven the different periods of education reform. Starting with a "survival-driven" phase of the 1960s and 1970s, where the sole goal was to raise school enrollment; to the more recent "ability-based, aspiration-driven phase" of the 1990s and 2000s, designed to fuel a knowledge-based economy—this relationship between educational objectives and future labor force needs has been both paramount and central to policymaking. If in the United States we posed the question of why we have a public education system, could we come up with as consistent an answer?

The clarity of intent in Singapore has also made it possible to construct a set of education institutions, each with a specific role to play in delivering against the system's over-arching objective. Many of our hosts described this clarity through the image of the "triangle of the

Singapore education system." At the top sits the Ministry of Education, responsible for setting policy, providing direction, and developing the national curriculum. The National Institute of Education (NIE), in a separate corner, is responsible for preparing the workforce—teachers, teacher leaders, school leaders and others—to deliver on the policy directions set by the Ministry. Finally, in the third corner sit the schools, the dominant execution arm responsible for delivering the initiatives set by the Ministry and providing feedback on the adequacy of the tools and workforce provided by the NIE and Ministry. These three entities deliver an ecosystem that individuals described as engendering strategic alignment with tactical empowerment. Simply put in a way that highlights the differences from our own system: the marching orders are clear and flow from a single source, while creativity and motivation are driven by perfecting the craft of high quality execution.

2. Sustained Focus

If the cadence of American education reform is often summarized by the refrain "this too shall pass," the Singaporean system is best characterized by the statement "this too shall last." Numerous speakers outlined four phases of development within the education system, each building upon the advances of the last. The first persisted from 1959 to 1978 with an emphasis on universal primary education and later universal lower secondary education. The next phase spanned 1979 to 1996 and was oriented around creating different education pathways to produce the range of required market-relevant skills. The third phase, from 1997 to 2011, repositioned the system to deliver the workforce needed to grow the knowledge-based economy. Singapore has recently launched a new era focused on teaching 21st century skills and character education, which the Ministry believes are required to produce more individuals capable of managing expanding companies and generating a more robust entrepreneurial sector. The duration of these phases is notable—the shortest lasted 14 years while the longest lasted nearly 20. Even in a relatively small system, indeed one that includes fewer schools and students than Massachusetts, sustained focus has been required to drive meaningful change. What might we achieve in this state if we set goals spanning decades rather than administrations?

3. Consistency of Communications

Ask Singaporeans to explain how the country's education system works, what factors have contributed to success, or what they are focused on currently and you will get the same set of phrases delivered with spellbinding consistency. Ask individuals about the specific steps they are taking to deliver on these catchphrases and they will produce a list of substantive actions currently underway. This is true from the top ranks of the Ministry and the NIE down to individual school leaders and teachers. First and foremost, these catchphrases focus on human capital—"people are our most important resource," and "our teachers are our nation builders"—setting a clear value base for the system. When asked how they are thinking about priorities, responses consistently reference the "new focus on citizenship and character education" as the hallmarks of the current reform phase. Finally, questions about failing schools consistently trigger the statement that "every school is a good school," a dominant perception that all schools have the ability to achieve value-added measures that are comparable, albeit for potentially different student populations. Five days into the echo chamber of speakers, one could not help but realize that not only is the direction clearly set and sustained, it is relentlessly communicated to all actors in the system using language that resonates with practitioners and ultimately becomes their own. Moreover, these are substantive ideas not empty phrases; teachers and administrators can provide concrete examples of their application.

4. A Top Quality Human Capital Management System

At its core, education is a human capital business with talent as the single most important input and salaries as the dominant expense; Singapore's extreme focus on constructing an elevated teaching profession reflects this reality. In business school, students typically take a course on human capital management that covers the major levers of a personnel system: recruitment, training, compensation, evaluation, and career paths. The architecture of human capital management in Singapore shows a full set of lessons across these levers. This begins with a focus on recruiting top talent: only the top third of students are eligible to become teachers, and then only around 20% of applicants are accepted into a teacher preparation program. Starting salaries are roughly comparable to those for entry-level engineers to allow the profession to attract a strong talent pool. Entrants progress through the national training program, which has been designed to reflect the reported needs of the Ministry and the schools. Three differentiated career ladders allow individuals to advance as master teachers, system leaders, or specialists, with new training conducted at each step along the way. All teachers are evaluated based on a mix of student development, collaboration with the community, support to colleagues, and contribution to the school; ratings are assigned based on a forced normal distribution and drive bonus and retention decisions. Each of these design choices is formatted to augment the others, yielding a rational and seemingly meritocratic professional infrastructure.

Perhaps even more striking is the way in which the human capital system has evolved to mimic that of many large corporations through intentional rotation. It is not unusual for top quality teachers to do rotations at the Ministry or the NIE to inform policy creation and teacher training; this facilitates feedback and ensures that the ideas of the Ministry and the NIE are properly informed by developments and conditions on the ground. Once an individual becomes a school leader, the expectation is that that leader will be reassigned to a new leadership post every 5-6 years, with the intent being for the leader to see different school environments, different student populations, and different grade levels. The emphasis on rotation creates a strong sense of system-wide accountability; realizing they are the custodians of an organization rather than independent actors, school leaders are disinclined to veer off strategy or seek disproportionate resources.

5. Incentivized Student and Parent Engagement

Within its education system, Singapore has a clear design for student and parent engagement that aligns both of these engines around the shared objective of producing the highest academic outcomes. The dominant mechanism that elicits this engagement is the Primary School Leaving Exam (PSLE) administered at the end of 6th grade, which is used to assign each student to a future education path. The exceptionally high stakes nature of this test generates anxiety for both parents and students, but also emphasizes the importance of total engagement from the start of a student's education experience. While the structure may not be a fit for our national context, it does raise the question of how in the US we drive student and parent engagement to align with the broader objectives of the K-12 system.

Final Reflections for an American Context

To be sure, Singapore has its problematic spots: the potential for a top-down system to be deaf to corrective feedback, early stage tracking, a de-emphasis of electives, anxiety among students and parents, and inequality that may grow with the burgeoning supplemental educational services industry. If public policy is, at its heart, a discipline of trade-offs, the United States will make different decisions. We will not design coherence top-down but will need to find bottom-up opt-in regimes that accomplish similar objectives. We will not mandate role definition or consolidate institutions, but will need to rely on incentive structures to send clear performance signals and align organizational behaviors. Yet these uniquely American strategies must seek to achieve the benchmarks of coherence that Singapore has in place: clear strategic priorities, consistent communication with sustained focus, a teaching profession capable of attracting and retaining the country's top talent, and methods for aligning parent and student engagement with the overarching priorities. While fragmentation within the U.S. is a challenge, it does not preclude states from setting an ambitious vision and then providing districts and teacher training institutions a set of Singaporean-style mechanisms that they could adopt in order to pursue this vision. Indeed, leading charter networks have already found ample room within the existing structure of policy incentives and autonomy conditions to create this style of coherence.

As the global economic system continues to morph at increasingly rapid rates, it seems hard not to believe that the states and countries capable of pivoting as the economy demands will see the greatest benefit for their citizens. Singapore serves as a pace horse; the country's deep-seated commitment to forward looking economic needs and an advanced ability to maneuver accordingly puts the challenge before us in stark repose.

LETTER 13. FIVE REFLECTIONS ON A THOUGHT-PROVOKING TRIP

— By Meghan O'Keefe
Vice President of Programs, Teach Plus

*An incredible trip – Coherence and clarity – Experience
across different levels of the system –
Clear pathways for teacher leadership – High
quality technical education pathways –
The question of individual choice*

Our trip to Singapore was incredible—both in terms of learning about the education system and in spending time with amazing colleagues who are all working to improve outcomes for students in Massachusetts. Over the few weeks since we've been back, I've reflected on a number of things:

1. **The remarkable coherence and clarity in Singapore's education system.** I know this was something that struck us all as critical to their success. We heard the same messaging from all levels of the system. Many of the ideas and concepts that we saw were ones that exist here in the United States, but the implementation here is often flawed and incomplete given the multiple layers of governance. It raised the question: Could such coherence be accomplished in an individual district, if not a whole state? There are still multiple stakeholders involved—district staff, unions, school staff, etc. —but it might be more realistic than state-wide coherence.

2. **The number of educators who have experience across different levels of the system.** We met quite a few people who had been teachers, principals, staff at the National Institute of Education, and who had worked at the Ministry of Education. That is much more unusual in the United States, where teachers and school leaders don't often have the opportunity to experience working at the district or state level. If they did, they would have a much better sense of why and how decisions are made, and school-level

perspectives would be included in those decisions more often. It could potentially be doable to create and run a program that gave people that opportunity in Massachusetts (for example, to arrange for a teacher to spend a year away from the classroom to work in a district office or the Department of Elementary and Secondary Education), if we could find a way to define very clear goals and outcomes of such a program.

3. **The incredibly clear pathways for teachers to leadership**. A graphic of the three different career pathways for teachers has stuck with me. While teacher leadership opportunities exist in various forms in the US (and nonprofits like Teach Plus are working to increase those opportunities), they tend to vary in quality and in accessibility, even as teacher leadership becomes a popular buzzword. Teachers who are working in one school or district might have access to a variety of opportunities to take on teacher leadership, while those in others might have none. There have been attempts at both the federal and state level to offer teacher leadership opportunities, but a number of things stand in the way. One is cost: Where does the money come from to train, support, and provide additional compensation for those in teacher leader roles? Another is definition: There has been resistance to defining teacher leadership too specifically at those levels, since districts and schools want to define "leadership" for themselves. However, the danger is that roles and responsibilities that don't have any connection to student learning get labeled as "teacher leadership," and when those efforts don't have any measurable impact, the education field moves on to the next appealing new idea.

What I think we can learn from Singapore regarding teacher leadership is to be very transparent about the opportunities that are available, and to provide support and professional development to help teachers be ready for those opportunities and to succeed in those roles. We know that leading other adults (as is included in many teacher leadership roles, whether it is leading a grade-level team or leading a school-wide initiative) is very different from teaching students, and it requires a different skill set. Providing access to training and support should be part of any teacher leadership program, as it is in Singapore.

4. **The seemingly high quality of the technical education pathways in Singapore.** My perception is that the quality of the career and technical education (CTE) options is more variable in the United States, and so some parents do not see CTEs as an acceptable option for their children. If the quality were consistently high and the pathway to a set of desirable 21st century jobs was clear as it is in Singapore, then American parents' perception might shift.

5. **The question of individual choice in a system like Singapore's is an interesting one.** Singapore won't end up with a glut of lawyers who can't find jobs because of their backwards mapping of economic and workforce need. However, that means that someone who really wants to be a lawyer might get turned away from that path and steered to another one. Individual career determination seems secondary to the greater good of the country, and that seems to be ingrained in the culture. It is difficult to imagine any level of the American government taking such a position, or its citizens going along with it.

Overall, it was a fascinating and thought-provoking trip, with many lessons that I am still mulling now that I am back in my everyday role. I look forward to thinking about next steps for Massachusetts.

LETTER 14. TEN LESSONS FROM SINGAPORE

— BY DAVID HARRIS
Deputy Director, Teachers21

A brief history of Singapore's growth and development –
Ten lessons to be learned from Singapore's education system –
Differences in context – What makes the system work –
Drawbacks of the Singaporean model

Singapore is a wildly successful young country, having emerged from poverty to become the 3rd highest per capita GDP in the world in its short 50-year history. In no small part, this success is due to its education system: international test scores that are consistently at the top; dropout rates that are appealingly low; and there are jobs for all graduates, with a national unemployment rate that hovers around 1%. Building on three earlier policy phases that focused on "survival," "efficiency," and "ability-driven" education, the fourth phase of the Singaporean education strategy is focused on "student-centered, values-based" education, and 21st century skills are a large part of that rhetoric. Indeed, there is plenty to learn from how Singapore approaches education, much of which they learned from the US and other school systems:

1. **Teachers as nation-builders**. Teachers are expected to be creators of knowledge, facilitators of learning, architects of learning environments, shapers of character, and leaders of educational change.

2. **Mastery focus with pathways for growth**. There are clear rubrics against which teachers are being measured (for example: the Current Estimate of Potential or CEP), and educators are given feedback three times a year on their progress. Students, too, are assessed in formative and summative ways, so students and parents know precisely where they stand and what they need to work on.

3. **Networked learning communities by subject, role, and professional interest.** Peers observe each other's classrooms, share teaching resources, and collaborate to improve their practice.

4. **Focus on values and socialization.** Learning processes are designed to put the community and the nation first in Singapore, communicating and modeling consistent values and norms, while respecting and embracing the four distinct cultures that make up the country. This aims to reduce inter-group tension and promote collaborative learning among students and teachers. For teachers, contributing to the profession through mentoring of novice teachers, collaborating, and modeling, is not only valued, but is also essential for professional advancement.

5. **Mother tongue education.** While English is the primary language in the country and is used in all content classes, it is required that each student learns his or her mother tongue (Malay, Mandarin, or Tamil) in school as well, which fosters respect for cultural differences.

6. **Principals are the key.** Principals are carefully selected and groomed, and are deeply trusted to tailor implementation of Singaporean values and policies to their school's context. In their final six months of pullout training (which occurs right before assuming a principalship), new leaders learn to be values-based, purposeful, innovative, and forward-looking in their roles of human resources leadership, strategic management, and in working in a complex environment. They also develop a global perspective fostered by continuous exposure to, and inquiry into, educational and economic systems from around the world. The fact that principals can be assigned to any school in the (albeit tiny) country, and are moved every 5-7 years, gives them the incentive to build school cultures that are not

principal-dependent and embody a consistent set of values and beliefs.

7. **Rethinking resources regarding class size.** John Hattie, in the 2008 book *Visible Learning for Teachers: Maximizing Impact on Learning*, pointed out that class size is not a key factor in student growth—instead, it is what happens in the class that drives growth. Singapore has chosen to allow class sizes to be large, but it invests heavily in technology, training, and support staff within each school so that the teaching practice maximizes student learning.

8. **Experimentation and assessment leading to broader adoption.** Innovation is encouraged, but broad-scale changes are only introduced after being researched and assessed in the context of the system-level goals. When new initiatives, such as professional learning communities (PLCs), are implemented on a broad scale, system leaders carefully communicate the what, the why, the when, and the who of the new policy or program, and consequently adoption is swift and highly impactful.

9. **Continuous improvement.** Every educator and leader speaks of continuous improvement—in their preparation, in their practice, in their partnerships, in their processes, and in the outcomes they produce.

10. **Coherence.** At the end of the day, it is the tight alignment of the vision, goals, and strategies throughout the system that ensures deep and lasting impact. To use an analogy: when all crewmembers row in the same direction, the boat flies along.

As we think about what relevance these lessons have for Massachusetts, we must think about differences in the two contexts. According to Singapore's National Institute of Education (NIE), Singapore is a small city-state consisting of 5.5 million people, 475,000 students (prior to their university, junior college and polytechnic institutes of higher education), 365 schools, 33,000 educators, and 34 students in an average class. They spent about 8.7 billion USD in 2013 (including for teacher training and across all branches of the ministry of education) or roughly $18,300 per student.

From its inception, Singapore has recognized education as one of—if not the most—important tools for building the nation. To Singapore, education is a non-negotiable *investment*, not an expense. The teaching profession is lauded, and earning a spot in the only teacher preparation program (run by the NIE which is a state agency) is highly competitive and requires high achievement, interviews, and demonstrations of the desired personal characteristics and values. Once selected, tuition is free, a job is guaranteed (although the Ministry of Education determines your placement), and salaries are comparable with that of engineers with the opportunity for bonuses exceeding 25% of base salary for top performers. Once on the job, teachers get 100 hours of professional development per year, a reduced workload in their first year (80% of a standard load), extensive mentoring from a senior teacher, and the ability to advance either as a lead teacher focused on pedagogy, a specialist in curriculum or other areas, or through the school leadership track.

What makes the system work—very much like for the best US charter networks—is the coherence within the system: everyone is committed to a single vision for student success (often written on the walls of the institution), the systems for developing and supporting teachers and school leaders are completely aligned, research-proven programs such as DuFours' Professional Learning Community work are implemented with a high degree of fidelity, administration is handled by business managers so the leadership can focus on instruction, there is autonomy within each school to tailor the curriculum and instruction to the student population, and the values they instill in the students are as important as their academic achievement. Also, much like teachers in successful charter networks, Singaporean teachers can expect to work 11 hours per day, must become expert in two subjects, and must be willing take on many extra duties beyond student loads of up to 200. It is perhaps no wonder that in this environment students outperform those in most other educational systems.

Besides tremendous workloads for teachers (that lead about 4% to leave each year, often when they start families) there are some other drawbacks to the Singaporean system and also some aspects of the system we might question. Singapore considers itself a meritocracy and uses high stakes (and therefore high stress) tests, particularly in the form of the Primary School Leaving Exam (PSLE). Taken at the end of 6th grade, the PSLE tracks students into different secondary schools. These secondary schools have different expectations, foci, and supports which allow the students' experience to be better tailored to their needs and their learning capacity—although once again these paths culminate in high stakes British General Certificate of Education (GCE) exams (N, O or A levels depending on the pathway). Many students and their parents rightly perceive that their opportunities are immediately limited at the age of 12. In all fairness, the system does allow late bloomers to transfer to faster tracks, much like our community colleges provide a pathway for some to enter four-year universities, although those transfers tend to be the exceptions not the rule. A side effect of the PSLE test has been the development of a tutoring industry that by some accounts makes up 3% of the country's GDP. If nothing else, this alone drives up the academic achievement of all students.

Compared with our system, Singapore does indeed seem to reach "struggling" students since their lowest performers on the Programme for International Student Assessment (PISA) tests still score higher than 70% of US students. The Singaporean objective is to have every student "achieve their full potential" (as opposed to "No Child Left Behind") although, with classes of 40 students and a style of instruction that emphasizes accuracy of content, few teachers seemed to be trained to support struggling learners or students with special needs. Moreover there is little time (1 hour per week) built in for any specialized instruction. There are actually a few special schools for those with extreme disabilities or those with consistently low academic performance, an approach the United States has chosen to eschew publicly (although the services are available privately), and one question that remains is the degree to which the pedagogy that is being developed to serve those special needs students will be applied more broadly in the future.

Perhaps the most common criticism of the system is the lack of focus on creativity and entrepreneurialism, but those are not the characteristics that have driven Singapore's success. Singapore has grown so dramatically because they look at where the global economy is going and then identify how they can fit in and drive that growth throughout Asia. They invest heavily in sending educators out to both learn about and support the growth of other countries, so that when those countries are looking for a partner to promote trade, Singapore is the obvious candidate. What Singapore does value is ensuring that every citizen has a meaningful job (migrants from Malaysia tend to fill in the really low level jobs) so education is geared to finding a suitable role for everyone. While perhaps limiting opportunity for some, this approach has reduced or even eliminated poverty and crime, and has allowed people from those four distinct cultures to coexist and thrive together while, in contrast, the American poverty gap continues to increase and racial tensions persist.

Letter 15. Learning from Singapore: Reflections from a Visit with a Delegation of Educators from Massachusetts

— By Fernando M. Reimers, EdD

Ford Foundation Professor of Practice in
International Education and Director of
Global Education Innovation Initiative,
Harvard Graduate School of Education

Admirable education features in Singapore –
What might we adopt in Massachusetts? –
Eight ideas for positive change

In this note I will do two things. First, I will distinguish several characteristics of Singapore's education system that I admire, and, second, I will discuss practices that educational institutions in Massachusetts might adopt, based on those characteristics that I admire. The two are different, for the latter requires that we think not only about Singapore's practices which may be contributing to the effectiveness of *their* education system, but also to think about the similarities and differences between the Singaporean and Massachusetts contexts, so that those practices might be transferred from one to the other with potentially similar effects. Not all things we admire in other nations transfer well and any process of educational transfer is, to some extent, a process of re-invention. There are certainly practices Singapore might also learn from Massachusetts, but discussing those is not the focus of this note.

Admirable education features in Singapore

Singapore's history is admirable in many ways that matter to the role education plays in that society. It is a history of how a small nation, which in five decades evolved from an impoverished former colony lacking in natural resources to a self-reliant nation highly dependent on knowledge intensive industries and trade. This development was a result of a firm commitment to the rule of law, competent government, and investment in education and other social policies. Political and education leaders often allude to the idea that the country's future and survival depends on cultivating the talent of each person, which makes education, the process designed to support such cultivation, central to the key narrative of the country and its future.

In addition to these overarching aspects of Singapore's historical development in which the narrative of education is embedded, eight distinctive features of education have contributed to the high performance of their education system. By high performance, I mean the capacity to achieve the goals that the leaders of the education system set out to achieve. Those goals have shifted over time, becoming more ambitious, and these shifts reflect four distinctive 'periods.' The first period had the goal of enrolling all students in school and teaching the basics (such as reading, writing, and essential math skills); second, the goal of getting all students to *complete* a course of basic education; third, the goal of fostering the development of high-order cognitive skills; and fourth, more recently, the goal of creating learning opportunities in schools for students to gain a broad range of cognitive and social competencies and to develop character and ethical values. These shifts in system priorities have reflected shifts in visions of policy elites regarding the economic and social imperatives facing the nation. It is the clarity with which these goals have been articulated and reframed, and the efficacy with which the Singaporean education system has been able achieve these goals, which makes the system high performing. A popular alternative to this conception of "high performing" makes reference to the achievement of students in various countries in comparative assessments of student knowledge and skills, such as the Programme for International Student Assessment (PISA). While the high levels of performance of Singaporean students on PISA would also make the country "high performing" by this definition, this is not an explicit goal of local education policy elites, and therefore it is not a consideration in my analysis.

1. A positive education narrative.

Education is highly valued in Singapore, and so are educators and the institutions in which they work. There are multiple manifestations of this, from the slogans painted on buses which say "Teachers, nation builders," to the way in which educators talk about their work. It is clear that education is believed to matter and this overarching belief is supportive of learning and teaching.

2. Education is a clear political priority of the State.

Education is not apolitical in Singapore. On the contrary, it is highly political and strategically political. This is reflected in the consistent and high level of priority education receives among government policies, including the financing of education. While education is perceived as a political priority for the nation's future, and perhaps because of it, there are limits to partisanship in education. This may be the result of the limited nature of political competition in Singapore, resulting from the dominance of the majority political party throughout most of the nation's history. Education is clearly a state-led activity; hence it is one of the avenues the state has to deliver services to the citizens, and to demonstrate its commitment to equal opportunity, fairness, and the rule of law. This policy priority assigned to education translates into financial support and conditions which attract and develop talented human resources in the sector.

3. There are clear and concise educational purposes in Singapore, aligned with future scenarios for the country's future development.

These goals are communicated often and are well known among educators at all levels of the education system. These goals are ambitious but communicated concisely and effectively.

Education is perceived to be an important contributor to the economic and social development of the nation, hence the state's intentionality of focusing on intended outcomes of education, in the form of knowledge, values, and skills, all of which align with national development goals. When these development goals change, so do education goals. Moreover, education leadership in Singapore includes the capacity to create conditions that allow education institutions to achieve their goals (which we might call leading for effectiveness), as well as the capacity to realign those goals (which we might call leading for relevance). To develop their capacity to lead for relevance, future school principals in Singapore are taught how to construct future scenarios, and they are asked to align various of these future scenarios for the nation with concomitant scenarios for schools of the future, and then asked to map a trajectory of improvement that can bring schools in the present towards the schools most aligned with desirable future scenarios.

4. **Education is viewed as a practice that depends on expert knowledge and this supports educator professionalism.**

Because education is highly valued in Singapore, and because schools attempt to reach ambitious goals for their students, it is understood that effective teaching is a complex practice that requires high levels of professionalism on the part of teachers and those who support them in developing practice aligned with expert knowledge. This view undergirds Singapore's efforts, including its linking of research and practice, its funding of education research, its conducting of such research in the same institution that is responsible for teacher and school leader professional development, the National Institute of Education, and in its giving practitioners an important role in generating that education research. The seamless continuum between research and practice that results from the fact that very often researchers at the National Institute of Education have spent significant periods as practitioners in classrooms, school leadership or in the Ministry of Education, as well as from the fact that often too practitioners in schools and in the Ministry, have spent stints at the National Institute of Education, makes the challenge of 'research utilization' less apparent in Singapore.

5. **Professional development is a very serious component of Singapore's education system.**

High levels of professional expertise, professionalism, are understood as the result of a continuous process of professional development. Education in Singapore is a learning profession not only in that it focuses on helping students learn, but also in the sense that those who practice it are always learning. Thus, learning is a central part of the way in which human resources— whether they are teachers, school administrators, or other professionals in the system—are managed and developed. For instance, teachers are evaluated yearly in ways which help guide professional development for the subsequent year as a way to help them reach their highest professional potential.

6. **There is much alignment and coherence among various education initiatives, and the various institutions of education appear to be tightly coupled.**

One gets the impression that in Singapore, the institutions of education are a veritable system of interlocking components, where the various elements of the system are synchronized with each other. This is greatly facilitated by the clear and concise nature of the goals that guide the system, and by the effective communication strategies which are deployed to ensure that all key stakeholders understand in what way their practice should align with those goals.

7. In Singapore education is a team sport.

The narrative of quality education in Singapore emphasizes the creation of organizational conditions that enable effective team performance, both in schools and between schools and other allied institutions, in order to produce excellence. Within schools, principals and other leaders foster collaboration among teachers in order to support coherence and consistent opportunities to learn for all students at all levels. Across schools and other institutions, education leaders support collaboration resulting in coherence and synergies. The virtuous tripartite relationship between schools, the ministry of education and the National Institute of Education is mentioned often as an example of such collaborative approach to leading improvement.

8. Singapore's educators are remarkably open to learning not only from each other, but from other countries as well.

Colleagues at the National Institute of Education are conversant with research and current education policy and practice in many different countries of the world, and they value the development of institutional relationships that foster intellectual exchange and collaboration. Education leaders also have an inquisitive mindset; they are always asking "How can we improve?" and "How can we do better?" There's little complacency among education leaders, in spite of the undisputed educational achievements of the nation.

What practices might we adopt in Massachusetts, inspired by Singapore's experience?

Which of these admirable practices might we adopt in Massachusetts? While the sizes of our populations are similar, our histories, politics, and institutional settings differ. Public education first emerged in the United

States almost two centuries ago in Massachusetts—which is to say that we are dealing with much older institutions and educational cultures and practices in this state than in Singapore. Unfortunate byproducts of such storied pedigree might be a certain conservatism, which might lead some in the State to be skeptical of the value of learning from others. Furthermore, the grassroots nature of our democratic politics also shape a strong tradition of local control of our schools, which can create real obstacles to system integration. In addition, the historical roots of our public schools in our democratic politics make for much more politicized educational practice than seems to be the case in Singapore. Local control by the people is somewhat at odds with the idea that education should be steeped in expert knowledge. In Massachusetts, it seems that we want our teachers to be expert, but we don't want experts to decide what should be taught, or maybe even who should teach. And, anyone with a vote in a town hall or in a school assembly feels entitled to advocating views about how schools should meet their objectives.

Typically, approaches to educational improvement fall in three distinct categories: a) Improving the performance of the existing system through the definition of standards and the use of incentives, b) Professionalizing the practice of education, and c) Promoting innovation and school redesign. While in practice many reforms reflect a blend of these approaches, it is most often the case that one of these approaches is dominant. In the United States, for example, standards-based reform has been the dominant approach to improvement for the last couple of decades, with some intermittent efforts to foster innovation and redesign, and relatively little attention to professionalizing education practice. In contrast, in Singapore, the dominant theory is clearly to professionalize educational practice to build a robust profession of educators (what is often termed in the country "the education fraternity").

In spite of these obvious differences in fundamental theories of change about educational improvement between Singapore and Massachusetts, there may be some practices we could re-examine in Massachusetts, inspired by Singapore's experience. Of course, we might also at some point tackle the adaptive challenge caused by the fact that standards-based reform might be inherently limited in its capacity to help schools become responsive to the quickly changing context of work and therefore become more relevant.

1. **Develop a positive education narrative.** We could establish concerted efforts to convey that education is indeed valued, as are teachers and public schools. Adopting a communication strategy that focuses on the many good education practices and achievements in the state would contribute to creating a climate where educators know they are indeed valued.

2. **Make education a more strategic priority in the future of the state**, although it would be challenging to make it strategically political and non-partisan. This would require investing in the formation of consensus among political, business, and civic leaders in the state regarding the role of education and the urgency to invest in the sector and to sustain high levels of professionalism.

3. **Align education goals with future scenarios for the country and State**. There have been efforts in Massachusetts to do this—the most evident of which are the development of the Massachusetts Curriculum Standards, important conversations that have taken place about assessment of student knowledge and skills (including the recent discussions of the Partnership for Assessment of Readiness for College and Careers [PARCC]), and the publishing of a 2008 report on education for the 21st century. But, our educational institutions, especially those involved in teacher and school leader preparation, could do a better job incorporating the discussion of the alignment between education goals and economic and social purposes into the curriculum, and there might be lessons we could learn

from Singapore in how that nation prepares its school leaders to develop a long term vision and how to lead for long term sustained improvement in their schools.

4. **Create a continuum of professional development.** With over 80 institutions involved in teacher preparation in Massachusetts, we have an abundance of riches in terms of professional development opportunities, particularly for initial teacher education. But such richness poses some challenges to coordination and coherence, and can hinder the agility with which our state can pivot teacher preparation to align it with new curriculum. We might learn from the extensive collaboration between Singapore's National Institute of Education and its K-12 schools in providing ongoing professional development to teachers. Might we create consortia of teacher preparation institutions and districts that collaborate in shaping a true continuum of professional development, from initial preparation to advanced practice?

5. **Create a *system* of teacher education.** Can we create a system of teacher education out of the current large group of largely independent institutions that achieves greater coherence and synergies in their various efforts? There are several mechanisms designed to promote such coordination, including those advanced by the Department of Elementary and Secondary Education, and the periodic meetings of Deans of Teacher Preparation Institutions. How might those convenings be leveraged to support efforts of institutional improvement in teacher preparation? Would it be possible to do for teacher preparation what the Massachusetts Department of Higher Education is doing to support college transfer across institutions through the creation of Transfer Pathways? Coordinating a series of convenings of chairs in core disciplines, the Department has facilitated the development of a consensus on general education

requirements, the exchange of course syllabi and instructional resources, and the development of expected learning outcomes in those subjects. Something similar could be done with great benefit specifically for initial teacher preparation programs.

6. **Invest more in the development of professional capacity.** If we are to achieve more coherence among our various educational initiatives designed to foster educational improvement, we would probably need to invest more in the development of professional capacity among school leaders and teachers, as it is in the school that these initiatives converge. We would also need to create coordination mechanisms among the various efforts advanced by an array of state agencies and independent organizations. This is a real adaptive challenge that would require an enabling political environment where partisanship is contained in order to create space for ambitious efforts at coordination, system integration, and attention to long-term outcomes.

7. **Education as a team sport.** With regards to Singapore's seventh feature, could we develop a narrative of quality education that emphasizes the team nature of the sport? In particular, this would require fostering a culture of collaboration in schools and districts, and across schools and other educational institutions, such as teacher preparation institutions.

8. **Always learning from others.** Lastly, our visit demonstrates that we can indeed hop on an airplane and visit another country to learn from her institutions and practices, and the reflections shared in these fifteen letters make explicit some of what we learned and allow us to share it with others. We should be able to make the comparative study of education a normal practice in our education and research institutions, and to cultivate and value the development of cross-national collaborations as much as our Singaporean colleagues do.

Appendix: The Authors

Lisa B. Battaglino, PhD

Lisa Battaglino is the Dean of the College of Education and Allied Studies at Bridgewater State University (BSU). She has played a key leadership role at BSU and has promoted the advancement of applicable technology including Propel-BSU, the first BSU tablet initiative, meaningful inner city public school partnerships, the development of projects focused on increasing Science, Technology, Engineering and Math (STEM) teachers in the region, and service-learning opportunities.

Prior to her role as dean, she spent 20 years as a special education professor and chairperson of the Special Education and Communication Disorders Department where she promoted the values of social justice, diversity, and inclusion by encouraging service through courses and in advocating for academic service in her role as the first service-learning faculty coordinator at BSU. Dr. Battaglino developed a thriving BSU partnership with the emerging country of Belize which has culminated in bringing Belizean undergraduate and graduate scholarship students to the BSU campus annually, and in bringing BSU students and faculty to Belize to work in many of the poorest schools in Central America. Dr. Battaglino has also conducted numerous workshops locally, nationally and internationally, offering information on how to include children with special needs into public school settings. In these ways and more, she has devoted her career to creating meaningful partnerships between public schools and universities through mutually beneficial collaborative programs and activities.

Connie K. Chung, EdD

Connie K. Chung is the Research Director for the Global Education Innovation Initiative at the Harvard Graduate School of Education—a research-practice-policy collaborative that works with education institutions in seven countries. Her field of research is in education for the 21st century, civic education, and global citizenship education, including building the capacity of organizations and people to work collaboratively toward providing a relevant, rigorous, meaningful education for all children that not only supports their individual growth but the development of their communities. She is the co-editor of the book, *Teaching and Learning for the Twenty-first Century: Educational Goals, Policies, and Curricula from Six Nations* (Harvard Education Press, 2016). In pursuing her research interest about the ways in which people from diverse backgrounds can learn to work together and leverage their collective power for positive change in their communities, she was involved in a multi-year, multi-site study of education reform and community organizing in the United States, the results of which are published in the book *A Match on Dry Grass: Community Organizing as a Catalyst for School Reform* (Oxford University Press, 2011).

In addition, Connie has worked as a staff member, consultant, and speaker with various human rights and civic education organizations. She currently serves on the board of two nonprofits, including Aaron's Presents, an organization that offers grants to students in grades 8 and below to encourage positive development for themselves and in their communities. A former public high school English teacher, she was nominated by her students for various teaching awards. She has taught as an adjunct lecturer on the topics of nonprofit management and multicultural education, and was also a curriculum consultant in the development of a K–12 global citizenship education curriculum. Dr. Chung received her B.A. in English Literature from Harvard College and her master's degrees in Teaching and Curriculum (1999) and in International Education Policy (2007) from the Harvard Graduate School of Education. Her doctorate is also from the Harvard Graduate School of Education.

MITALENE FLETCHER, PhD

Mitalene Fletcher is Director of PreK-12 and International Programs for Harvard Graduate School of Education's Programs in Professional

Education (PPE). Her work involves developing institutes for education leaders through a portfolio that includes the Think Tank on Global Education as well as Equity, Quality, and Leadership in Education, which is a program exclusively for the professional development of UNICEF education officers. Both of these are chaired by Professor Fernando Reimers. Through PPE, Fletcher serves on the faculty of the Management Development Program (MDP), co-teaching a module on the internationalization of higher education.

Fletcher began her career teaching secondary school in Toronto, Canada. Before coming to Harvard, she was program director for the Paul A. Kaplan Center for Educational Drama at New York University (NYU), where she designed and managed a suite of graduate courses and teacher development programs that introduced interactive, arts-based strategies into classrooms at all levels of schooling. Fletcher received a Ph.D. in international development and education from NYU, where her research focused on the reorganization of teacher education in democratic South Africa. Mitalene holds a Bachelor of Arts. (Hons) and a Bachelor of Education from Queen's University in Canada.

DAVID HARRIS

David Harris is Deputy Director of Teachers21 where he is responsible for strategic planning, business development, finance, and operations. He consults with schools, districts, and other not-for-profit leaders on business strategy and organization. Previously, he was an education leadership consultant working with school districts and education-related service organizations to develop strategies aimed at improving outcomes for more students. Projects involved assessing professional development needs, school culture, public-private partnerships, and potential applications of technology.

David received his School Superintendent license in Massachusetts in May 2011 after serving in Needham Public Schools. Prior to that, he was Managing Director of the nonprofit UPCS Institute, which created and delivered leadership and classroom instruction to 200 urban and rural Early College High Schools nation-wide. David also spent six years in the classroom as an 8th grade math teacher.

Before earning a Master of Art in Teaching (MAT) from Simmons College and entering the education field, David spent 20 years as a senior executive, product marketing director and strategy consultant in various computer software and retail organizations. David holds an MBA from Harvard Business School and a Sc.B. in Biochemistry from Brown University.

JOEY LEE

Joey Lee is the Education Programs Manager at Education First (EF), a family-owned global education organization whose North American headquarters is in Cambridge, MA. Joey contributes to the educational programming for professional learning, global student leadership summits, and weshare, EF's digital learning platform. He joined EF from Pinkerton Academy in Derry, NH where he served as a cultural geography teacher, curriculum coordinator, and teacher mentor in the social studies department, in addition to directing the Chinese exchange program and serving as the hockey coach. Joey is the New Hampshire Department of Education's 2014 Teacher of the Year.

VANESSA LIPSCHITZ

Vanessa Lipschitz joined the Jacobson Family Foundation in September 2014 as the Portfolio Manager for the foundation's education work. In this role, she is responsible for identifying potential grantees as well as providing strategic planning and advisory support to current grantees. The Jacobson Family Foundation's education portfolio is focused on providing support to schools, educational programs, and other initiatives that seek to achieve student academic outcomes that push beyond proficiency to performance levels that are internationally competitive.

Prior to joining the foundation, Vanessa was a Project Leader at the Boston Consulting Group (BCG) where she worked with both for-profit and nonprofit clients on projects primarily focused on strategy development. At BCG, Vanessa had the opportunity to work with Fortune 500 companies in the retail and financial services sectors. About half of Vanessa's work was focused on the social and public sector, including projects for government agencies, academic institutions, and foundations. Vanessa also spent three years at TDC, a management consulting firm, working exclusively with nonprofit organizations on strategic planning, new business planning, and organizational redesign. At TDC, Vanessa's clients included education organizations as well national parks, museums and other social service providers. Vanessa began her career at Rhode Island Kids Count, where she assisted with research and data analysis in the areas of education and childcare.

Vanessa received a Bachelor of Arts in Economics and Public Policy from Brown University. She also holds an MBA from Harvard Business School and an MPP from the Harvard Kennedy School.

EE-LING LOW, PHD

Ee-Ling Low is Head of Strategic Planning & Academic Quality at the National Institute of Education, Singapore. She was the Associate Dean of Teacher Education from 2009 to 2013. She obtained her PhD in Linguistics (Acoustic Phonetics) from the University of Cambridge, UK under the University's Overseas Graduate Scholarship award. She won the Fulbright Advanced Research Scholarship in 2008 which she spent at the Lynch School of Education in Boston College. She played a leading role in the conceptualization of the NIE Strategic roadmap: towards 2017 and the development of the Teacher education for the 21st century (TE21) model. In 2012, she was awarded the Public Administration Medal (Bronze) by the President of the Republic of Singapore. She is Singapore's representative in Stanford University's International Teacher Policy Study and Harvard Graduate School of Education's Global Education Innovation Initiative.

David Lussier, EdD

David Lussier is the Superintendent of Wellesley Public Schools. David was a high school history teacher in Massachusetts, where he earned National Board Certification and was named the Massachusetts Teacher of the Year in 2000. As a White House Fellow, David later served as Associate Director of Domestic Policy in the Clinton and Bush Presidential Administrations and participated in the development of the *No Child Left Behind Act*. After leaving the White House, David joined the National Board for Professional Teaching Standards (NBPTS), where he served as a policy advisor to the president and later as research director. Prior to coming to Wellesley, David was the Executive Director of Educator Quality for the Austin Independent School District. David earned a Bachelors Degree in History from the University of Massachusetts Lowell, a Master of Arts in Teaching from Boston University, and Master's and Doctoral Degrees in educational leadership from the Harvard Graduate School of Education.

Christine B. McCormick, PhD

Christine B. McCormick has been the Dean of the College of Education at the University of Massachusetts Amherst since 2005. She received her Ph.D. in educational psychology, with a minor in measurement and statistics, from the University of Wisconsin-Madison. Previously, she was a faculty member and held administrative roles at the University of New Mexico and the University of South Carolina where she taught graduate and undergraduate courses in human growth and development, educational psychology, learning and cognition, and classroom assessment.

Dr. McCormick is the author or coauthor of publications on a variety of topics in child development and education, including research on metacognition and cognitive strategies. Her publications include chapters on metacognition published in the *Handbook of Psychology*, 1st and 2nd Editions, published by John Wiley & Sons and in the *Educational Psychology Handbook,* published by the American Psychological Association. She also co-authored several textbooks with Michael Pressley, including *Child and Adolescent Development for Educators* and *Educational Psychology: Learning, Instruction, Assessment.*

Dr. McCormick has served three-year terms on the executive boards of the Council of Academic Deans from Research Education Institutions (CADREI), an assembly of deans of education from research and land grant institutions throughout North America, and of the American Educational Research Association's Organization of Institutional Affiliates. She was also appointed by Governor Deval Patrick to the Massachusetts Special Commission on Civic Engagement and Learning, which completed its work in January 2013. Dr. McCormick has served on the editorial boards of two major journals in her field: *The Journal of Educational Psychology* and *Educational Psychology Review* and is a Fellow of the American Psychological Association.

E. B. O'Donnell

Eleanor (Nell) O'Donnell is a doctoral student at the Harvard Graduate School of Education and an education consultant. She has over ten years of experience working with nonprofit organizations, international non-governmental organizations, and schools. Her particular areas of interest include the impact of parental beliefs on their children's education, early childhood care and education, emergent literacy and numeracy, global education, and curriculum development. She earned a Bachelor of Arts in International Studies and French from Washington University in St. Louis, Missouri and a Master of Education in International Education Policy from the Harvard Graduate School of Education in Cambridge, MA.

Meghan O'Keefe

Meghan O'Keefe is the Vice President of Programs at Teach Plus, a national nonprofit which empowers teachers to take leadership over key policy and practice issues that affect their students' success. Before joining Teach Plus at its founding to lead its T3 (Turnaround Teacher Teams) Initiative, Meghan was the Project Director for School Turnaround Strategies at Mass Insight, where she provided overall project management and partner development for programs in Mass Insight's school turnaround focus area. Prior to Mass Insight, she held positions as the Director of Strategic Planning and the Director of Operations in the New York City Department of Education's Student Enrollment office, and taught second grade for several years. She earned a Master of Business Administration from the Yale School of Management, a Bachelor of Arts from Boston College, and a Master of Education from Lesley College as part of the Lesley-Shady Hill School Teacher Training Program.

FERNANDO M. REIMERS, EdD

Fernando Reimers is the Ford Foundation Professor of Practice in International Education and the Director of both the Global Education Innovation Initiative and of the International Education Policy program at the Harvard Graduate School of Education. An expert in the field of global education, his research and teaching focus on the relationship between education policy, innovation, leadership, and quality improvement to support children and youth in developing the skills they need to thrive in the 21st century. His current research focuses on the study of educational policies and programs that develop 21st century competencies through a cross-national study focused on Chile, China, Colombia, India, Mexico, the United States, and Singapore. He has also studied the impact of entrepreneurship education with youth in the Middle East and the impact of citizenship education on youth in Latin America.

Dr. Reimers is the founding director of the International Education Policy masters program at the Harvard Graduate School of Education, a program focused on the development of innovative leaders who are committed to expanding global educational opportunity. He advises governments, international development organizations, foundations, and private groups that are working to advance a global system to empower all children to become architects of their own destinies. He serves on numerous boards of educational organizations, including the Massachusetts Board of Higher Education, and the US Commission for UNESCO. In 2015 he was distinguished with the appointment as the CJ Koh Visiting Professor of Education at the National Institute of Education of Singapore.

OON-SENG TAN, PHD

Tan Oon-Seng is Director of the National Institute of Education (NIE), Singapore. He was previously Dean of Teacher Education at NIE where he spearheaded the Teacher Education for the 21st Century (TE21) initiative as a major milestone innovation for teacher education both nationally and internationally. Professor Tan was President of the Asia-Pacific Educational Research Association (APERA, 2008-2010) and the Vice-President (Asia and Pacific Rim) of the International Association for Cognitive Education and Psychology (IACEP, 2008-2011). He is currently Editor-in-Chief of the Educational Research for Policy & Practice (ERPP) journal and Lead Editor of the Asia Pacific Journal of Education (APJE). Professor Tan was a winner of The Enterprise Challenge (TEC) Innovator Award in Singapore for co-pioneering a project on Innovation for the Knowledge-based Economy. In 2014, he was conferred the Public Administration Medal (Silver) by the President of the Republic of Singapore for his dedication and achievement in the field of education.

PAUL F. TONER

Paul F. Toner, is the Founder of Cambridge Strategic Partnerships, an education consulting firm. He is the former president of the 113,000-member Massachusetts Teachers Association (MTA). Toner, a middle school social studies teacher, lawyer, and former president of the Cambridge Education Association, was elected MTA president after serving for four years as the association's vice president. He left office on July 14, 2014.

As an educator and teacher leader, Toner has been a strong advocate for students and educators. He has been an avid promoter of teacher leadership and for improving student achievement through labor management collaboration at the district, state, and national levels.

Toner graduated from Boston University's College of Liberal Arts with a bachelor's degree in political science and international relations. He also holds a master's degree in secondary education from the University of Massachusetts in Boston. While teaching full time, Toner earned his juris doctorate from Suffolk University Law School at night. He is also a teacher leader fellow from the Pahara-Aspen Institute Fellowship Program, part of the Aspen Global Leadership Network.

ELEONORA VILLEGAS-REIMERS, EdD

Eleonora Villegas-Reimers, EdM, EdD is the Chair of the Department of Elementary and Special Education and a faculty member at Wheelock College where she has worked since 1988. She has served as the Dean of the School of Education and Child Life, Acting Dean of the Child and Family Studies Division, Chair of the Elementary Department, Coordinator of the Child Development and Early Childhood Program, and Coordinator of the Child Development Studies Program.

Dr. Villegas-Reimers was prepared as a teacher in her home country of Venezuela, and completed her graduate education at the Harvard Graduate School of Education: a master's of education with a focus on counseling, and a doctorate of education with a focus on human development. She currently serves on the State Board of the Department of Early Education and Care, the Universal Pre-Kindergarten Taskforce created by Boston Mayor Walsh, and the Boston Public School (BPS) Countdown to Kindergarten Steering Committee. She has also recently served on the Educator Preparation Advisory Group to the State Secretary of Education, the BPS Teacher Diversity Workgroup, and the BPS Panel of Experts on Literacy to advise the Boston Mayor and BPS superintendent. In 2009, she also served as a member of the English

Language Learners sub-committee of the Massachusetts Board of Elementary and Secondary Education's Committee on the Proficiency Gap. In addition, Dr. Villegas-Reimers has worked as a consultant to a number of international organizations, including UNESCO, the World Bank, the Inter-American Development Bank, the Board on International Comparative Studies of the National Research Council, and the Academy for Educational Development on matters related to education, teacher preparation and development, education for democracy, and multiculturalism.

ACKNOWLEDGEMENTS

This project was made possible thanks to the generous support and committed citizenship of many individuals and institutions. We appreciate the different ways in which each of the institutions of the participants in the delegation enabled each of us to visit Singapore. We are in debt to Professor Oon Seng Tan, director of the National Institute of Education, and to his colleagues for their partnership and generous hospitality during the visit. We are grateful for the enthusiastic thought partnership of Dr. Susan Lane from the Department of Higher Education, from helping to invite leaders of schools of education in Massachusetts, develop a focus for the visit, to the preparation of this document and of a plan to make the learnings from this visit useful to ongoing efforts in Massachusetts. We are also appreciative for the helpful stewardship and conversations with Dr. Heather Peske from the Department of Elementary and Secondary Education, for her help in developing the focus for the visit. We appreciate the financial support of the Nellie Mae Foundation, and the thought leadership of the Foundation's President Nick Donohue. We thank Education First Vice-President Kate Berseth and her colleagues for the enthusiastic response to this initiative and for the excellent organization of the visit. We are grateful to Nell O'Donnell for her excellent coordination of the academic program with our colleagues at the National Institute of Education and for her superb editing of this document. We appreciate the enthusiasm and guidance of Nigel Lee, CEO at Lulu, and of Daniel Berze at Glass Tree Academic Publishing, and the professionalism of their colleagues who worked on the publication of this book. Their ongoing innovations in the publishing industry will enable us to engage a wide group of colleagues in the dialogue and collective action necessary to professionalize teaching and support 21st century education.